CONTENTS

TRACING YOUR FEMALE ANCESTORS

A Guide for Family Historians

Adèle Emm

Pen & Sword
FAMILY HISTORY

First published in Great Britain in 2019
PEN & SWORD FAMILY HISTORY
an imprint of
Pen & Sword Books Ltd
Yorkshire — Philaddelphia

Copyright © Adèle Emm, 2019

ISBN 978 1 52673 013 8

A CIP catalogue record for this book is
available from the British Library.

Typeset in Palatino and Optima by CHIC GRAPHICS

Printed and bound in England by TJ International Ltd Padstow Cornwall

Pen & Sword Books Ltd incorporates the imprints of Pen & Sword
Airworld, Archaeology, Atlas, Aviation, Battleground, Discovery, Family
History, Fiction, History, Maritime, Military, Military Classics, Politics,
Select, Social History, True Crime, Frontline Books, Leo Cooper,
Remember When, Seaforth Publishing, The Praetorian Press,
Wharncliffe Local History, Wharncliffe Transport,
Wharncliffe True Crime and White Owl.

For a complete list of Pen & Sword titles please contact

PEN & SWORD BOOKS LTD
47 Church Street, Barnsley, South Yorkshire, S70 2AS, England
E-mail: enquiries@pen-and-sword.co.uk
Website: www.pen-and-sword.co.uk
or
PEN & SWORD BOOKS LTD
1950 Lawrence Rd., Havertown, PA 19083, USA
E-mail: Uspen-and-sword@casematepublishers.com
Website: www.penandswordbooks.com

Contents

PREFACE

What women take for granted today; access to the professions, equal pay (still under discussion), equal opportunities (ditto), universal healthcare, safe childbirth and ownership of property was, for our grandmothers and great grandmothers, wishful thinking. In many northern cities more women had jobs, albeit unskilled, than their husbands but still juggled responsibility for a large family, cooking, household cleaning and laundry.

A woman took her father's surname at birth, her husband's on marriage and was formally identified by his initials. Should a spouse die, widows and widowers often remarried through necessity of child care and financial support. Each successive marriage produced more children, making it difficult to unravel the female side of our family tree.

Society has come a long way, and this book follows the path travelled by our female ancestors, both the privileged minority and their working-class sisters. It covers the period from 1815, when Britain was plunged into economic crisis following the end of the Napoleonic Wars, to 1914, the start of the First World War, an event which irrevocably changed everyone's lives, especially women's.

The aim of this book is to enhance understanding of great grandma's daily life and legacy, understand her battles and suggest genealogical sources.

The women's branch of a family tree is known as the distaff side. A distaff? The stick holding flax or wool when spinning, and spinning was the woman's task in life …

NOTE ON MONEY

Prior to decimalisation in 1971, monetary units were pounds (£), shillings (s) and pence (d); twenty shillings to the pound and twelve pence to the shilling. There were four farthings (¼d) or two halfpennies (pronounced ha'penny, ½d), to one penny (1d). Ledgers recorded figures as £1 10 6 signifying £1 10 shillings and 6 pence. For amounts under £1, I have written it thus: 10s 6d (10 shillings and 6 pence) although our grandparents might also write it as 10/6; whole shillings as 10/-. Decimalisation reconfigured 240 old pence into 100 new pence; ten old shillings became 50p and one shilling 5p. £1 was worth considerably more than today.

Web addresses were correct at the time of writing. Subscription sites like Ancestry, FindMyPast and TheGenealogist constantly update records, please keep checking them.

ACKNOWLEDGEMENTS

Many people helped me to research this book. Thanks are especially due to: Simon Fowler; Rupert Harding; Katie Henderson, Museum Officer, Manchester Police Museum; Sally Jastrzebski-Lloyd, Manager, Elizabeth Gaskell's House, for permission to reproduce Elizabeth Gaskell's passport; Tony Lees, Archives Officer, Archives and Local History, Manchester Central Library; Margaret Myerscough, Senior Librarian, and staff at Stockport Heritage and Archives. Finally, I must add my appreciation to the public library service constantly beleaguered by financially strapped local councils. Long may you survive.

Chapter 1

BIRTH, MARRIAGE AND DEATH

According to family myth, we were 'diddled out' of Tickford Abbey in Newport Pagnell because 'there were only girls'. I dismissed this as far-fetched until I discovered an 1840s family with four daughters, Hooton, the same surname as the builders and original owners of the Abbey. The law of primogeniture, where an estate and inheritance is passed to the firstborn male, was crucial and explains Henry VIII's obsessive craving for a legitimate son. In aristocratic and privileged circles with an estate to inherit, brothers, no matter in which order they were born, inherited before sisters and the son of a deceased elder brother had precedence over everyone else. It wasn't until the 1925 Administration of Estates Act (England and Wales) that this was addressed.

Put simply, boys were more important than girls.

BIRTH
Giving birth was incredibly dangerous for a woman regardless of her status in society, Queen Victoria included. Even though the medical fraternity underplayed the danger by claiming it was 'only six to seven per cent' who didn't survive, many a literate wife wrote a fond farewell letter to her husband in case she died.

Unlike today, there wasn't a reliable form of contraceptive and each successive pregnancy increased the risk of a woman's death. The first viable form of family planning other than abstinence was Charles Goodyear's 1839 invention of rubber vulcanisation and, from the late 1850s, mass-production of rubber condoms. This reusable thick-seamed sheath was unconducive to harmonious

1

relations with a naïve wife, but prevented rakish men contracting venereal disease from prostitutes. Family planning as we know it today was the mission of Marie Stopes (1880–1958), only really taking off post the First World War.

The fashionable management of a woman in a 'delicate condition' in the early half of the nineteenth century was to be bled by leeches and follow a strict diet, thus ensuring a smaller baby and subsequently easier delivery.

Such was the treatment ministered in 1817 to Princess Charlotte, the only child of the Prince Regent (later George IV), who, according to the *Oxford Journal*, 1 November 1817, rose at nine, breakfasted with her husband, Prince Leopold, and spent much of her time resting in a garden chair. So thrilled was the populace by her pregnancy, betting shops speculated on the gender of the forthcoming child. She went into labour at Claremont House but, when baby was diagnosed as transverse, the doctors dithered about the delivery. After fifty hours of labour and no painkiller, the poor woman gave birth to a 9lb stillborn son. Still haemorrhaging from medical mismanagement (forceps were out of favour) and convulsions, she too died. She was 21.

Queen Victoria's first child, daughter Princess Victoria (1840–1901) was born following a twelve-hour labour and only her last two out of nine, Prince Leopold (1853–84) and Princess Beatrice (1857–1944), were born with the aid of a new technology, chloroform. Following her physician's 1858 publication of the ground-breaking book, *On Choloroform and Other Anaesthetics* (see *https://archive.org/details/onchloroformothe1858snow*), Dr John Snow (1813–58) ensured pain relief in childbirth was finally a reality – for the privileged.

If death and acute pain occurred in royal circles, imagine how much worse it was for an ordinary woman. Breech births were dangerous complications (as now) and if a doctor resorted to a caesarean, the mother usually died. Doctors and fathers faced an impossible decision; save mother or baby. At a time when some barbaric implements were used to extract foetuses and babies, both

Memorial to Mary Madden who died in childbirth 26 February 1830 and son Frederick who died aged five days. St George's Church, Bloomsbury.

mother and infant usually died. Once baby was delivered, there was the danger of afterbirth, possible haemorrhaging and infection. An infant's name appearing on a gravestone with its mother, or a child registered as 'male' or 'female', was a child who died at or shortly after birth.

Only the middle class and gentry had access to physicians. Everyone else resorted to family members, mother, mother-in-law or local midwife (old English *mid* 'with' and *wif* 'woman'; with the woman). Synonyms for giving birth included lying-in, accouchement (an *accoucheur* was a male midwife, first known use 1727), parturition, childbed, birthing, confinement and travail.

In 1877, Thomas Bull published his 26th edition of *Hints to Mothers for the Management of Health during the Period of Pregnancy and in the Lying-in-Room*. It advised on diet, morning sickness, prevention of miscarriage, labour, management post childbirth, wet and dry nursing and weaning. He recommended new mothers lie recumbent for at least four days, warning, 'Among the poorer classes of society, who get up very soon after delivery, and undergo much fatigue, the "falling down of the womb" is a very common and distressing complaint'. His suggestion, 'a bandage, wide enough to cover the whole length of the abdomen, is to be applied directly after delivery', adding this was especially useful for women with many children in quick succession or who are 'short and stout'. An indirect reference to Queen Victoria perhaps?

The middle classes employed monthly nurses for the lying-in period of four weeks following birth.

For the working class, there was no prissy rest and relaxation whilst pregnant or after delivery. Mum worked up to the delivery date, returning as soon as possible after the birth. Only in 1891 was a law passed (Factory and Workshop Act) prohibiting factory owners employing women within four weeks of childbirth. It applied to women working in factories but two years later was extended to eleven weeks after birth for all working mothers.

Wet nursing was commonplace, especially for the gentry who considered breastfeeding distasteful. Middle- and upper-class babies could be sent away for up to three years until fully weaned. Both wet and dry nursing were frowned on by the medical fraternity concerned with appalling neo-natal and childhood death rates. Dry nursing was putting a baby to a non-lactating breast for comfort whilst feeding baby whatever solid food was available. In 1862, physician M.A. Baines complained 'fashionable' wet and dry nursing was 'most disastrous in a sanitary and social point of view'.

A wet nurse had to be acquired, often a woman who had just lost her baby. It was not well paid. The more privileged demanded a superior wet nurse. Before confinement and on behalf of his patient, physicians advertised in local newspapers for a respectable married woman with several children willing to take on another. Respondents applied by letter which implied literacy. Wet nurses also advertised themselves through this medium and word of mouth, plus local knowledge was useful to both parties.

In the tragic case of Princess Charlotte, the Royal Physician Sir Richard Croft interviewed a married woman with three children for a position offering an extraordinary salary. Her children were medically examined to check they, too, were fit and healthy. For reasons of discretion, he and his colleagues spoke French during the interview not realising the (unnamed) prospective wet nurse understood – she informed them part way through the interview. On 1 November 1817, the *Leicester Chronicle* reported the remuneration – for a prince, a one-off payment of £1,500 plus £200 a year. It admitted not knowing the fee should Princess Charlotte deliver a daughter.

Why did Sir Richard Croft go to such lengths in choosing a wet nurse? Survival rates for a wet nurse's own baby and the child she was nursing were appalling. In 1859, 184,264 children under the age of 5 died. This represented two in five deaths that year for all ages; 105,629 were under 1 – a total infant mortality of 45 per cent. Several reasons were advocated. Protesting this figure was higher than for animals, Sir Arthur Leared, Physician to the Great Northern Hospital, Manchester, blamed young women and mothers for working in factories, accusing them of abandoning children for money. An educated privileged man, he ignored or was not apprised of the fact that many worked through sheer necessity, especially if their husbands were unemployed. However, supporting his theory, infant mortality fell during the Lancashire Cotton Famine (1861–5) – it was assumed because women were forced to stay at home and directly care for their children.

Another explanation for low infant survival was diet. Godfrey's Mixture or Cordial, a brew containing laudanum and treacle with the dual benefit of filling baby's tummy and sedating it at the same time, was popular with mothers in the textile industry. Also, during the mid-1800s food was heavily adulterated, especially milk and

Hetty and Albert Harris, 1913. Author's collection © Adèle Emm

bread which inadvertently poisoned wet nurse, mother and infant, sometimes causing the death of all. In the workhouse, babies often received totally unsuitable – but cheap – food.

Today, baby blues, or postnatal depression, is well recognised. Our ancestors regarded it as a form of insanity and/or melancholia. Should a female ancestor be admitted to an asylum a few months after childbirth, this could have been the cause. Bethlem Hospital Archives (*http://museumofthemind.org.uk*) include photographs of named women treated for insanity following postnatal depression, infidelity, over-work, alcoholism, senile dementia, anxiety and epilepsy etc. A psychiatric hospital since 1247, it allows personal visits by appointment and some records are accessible via FindMyPast (*www.findmypast.co.uk/bethlem*).

A surviving family Bible is a cherished source of dates for births, marriages and deaths. In the latter half of the nineteenth century, announcing a birth in the personal columns of the local paper became popular even for those of a less moneyed background. Once the cost of photography was within the reach of ordinary folk, it became widespread from the 1880s for mother and baby to have their photograph taken in the nearest studio, usually around the christening date. Such photographs are common in family albums; the trick, of course, is recognising who they are.

Illegitimacy

Up to civil registration 1 July 1837 and beyond, baptisms were recorded in the parish register. If there's no name in the father's column, the baby was illegitimate. For a few years after civil registration, not everyone understood children had to be registered separate from baptism so, for a while, some births are only found as christenings in the church register.

If, after 1837 there was no name in the father's column of the birth certificate, it's also highly likely the child was illegitimate. Children could be registered without parents being married so you may find parents married after a baptism – or not. My great great grandmother was pregnant with her third child when she married,

1857, in Manchester Cathedral some seven miles from where she actually lived. I've always assumed she didn't want neighbours to know her children were illegitimate, with the stigma that afforded. Her first child was known under both her maiden and married surname.

As the nineteenth century progressed, so did the stigma attached to illegitimacy and unmarried motherhood. It's estimated that by the middle of the century, 7 per cent of children were illegitimate and 20 to 30 per cent of brides pregnant on their wedding day. An illegitimate child could not inherit. Even if an illegitimate child's parents married after its birth (changed under the 1926 Legitimacy Act), this child was *filius nullius* (Latin; child of no one) and would not inherit, although their descendants could. As current law stands, they still cannot unless specifically named in a will or the father's name is recorded on the birth certificate.

In 1860, following the brutal murder in Whitechapel of Mary Emsley, property owner of more than 100 properties in her own name, there was considerable speculation in *The Times* that, as a 'bastard' (she was actually legitimate), her estate was forfeit to the crown. Thrice-married Mrs Emsley had borne no children herself but the squabble over her considerable estate continued well into the next decade, as explained in Sinclair McKay's *The Mile End Murder: The Case Conan Doyle Couldn't Solve* (2017).

I've seen the following in parish baptism registers both pre and post 1837: 'baseborn', 'illegitimate', 'bastard' and 'whoreson' – no political correctness in those days. Other euphemisms include 'born out of wedlock', 'left hand', 'misbegotten' and 'bye-blow'. It was statistically less common for an illegitimate child to be baptised, which compounded the stigma. For elusive records prior to 1837 (and for anyone who didn't realise they still had to register their child) online parish clerks, where volunteers transcribe records, may be found for free. Try *www.ukbmd.org.uk/online_parish_clerk*. The Church of the Latter Day Saints website, also free, is another resource (*www.familysearch.org*) but you must register; *www.freereg.org.uk* is worth checking. Local libraries have parish records on microfilm, books and transcriptions. As always, aim to see originals because transcribers make errors and omissions, sometimes ignore handwritten marginal nuggets (e.g. accusing men of paternity) and, in the case of weddings, witnesses, parental occupations etc. are often omitted.

Of course, if a wife conceived another man's child, it's technically illegitimate but, if she were discreet, without today's DNA tests it might never be exposed.

Illegitimacy was an inconvenience (an understatement) for a nineteenth-century child, but a woman pregnant before marriage, especially a middle- or lower-middle-class girl where purity was prized, risked ostracism. Pregnancy was condoned by provincial villagers if a couple married quickly and consequently had the child within wedlock; plenty of my Wiltshire and Buckinghamshire ancestors had her first child four or five months after the wedding.

A middle-class girl who found herself pregnant, however, may have been thrown out of her parent's house. Following the 1913 Mental Deficiency Act, some committed their daughter to an insane asylum (urban legend suggests this happened prior to 1913) because only a mad woman had a sexual liaison before marriage.

A pregnant servant could be dismissed instantly without a character even if the putative father was master of the house or fellow servant. With no reference, it was virtually impossible to find a respectable job and consequently her only recourse was prostitution and/or the workhouse. Pregnant shop assistants faced the same fate.

Sisters Emily and Louise Turner were shop-girls at William Whiteley's eponymous Westbourne Grove store in London (*www. whiteleys.com/history*). Although married and espousing Victorian respectability and values, Whiteley (1831–1907) enjoyed fraternising with pretty employees younger than himself. On 10 April 1879, Emily (aged about 22 to Whiteley's 48) gave birth to a son and, moving in with a friend, George Rayner, registered Horace George Rayner as his child.

Nearly thirty years later, 24 January 1907, William Whiteley now

75, was shot dead outside his office. Pleading insanity as Whiteley's unacknowledged illegitimate son, Horace George Rayner alias Turner, was arrested at the scene. Devoured by the contemporary press, the sensational story unravelled during the Old Bailey trial on 18 March, see *www.oldbaileyonline.org* and British Newspaper Archive (BNA) *www.britishnewspaperarchive.co.uk*.

Not only had Emily had a child by Whiteley, but so had younger sister Louise; Cecil Whiteley was born in 1885. Having joined the store in 1882, Louise lived at 13 Greville Road, Kilburn, 'under Mr Whiteley's protection' from January 1883 until a disagreement in May 1888. She never saw him again.

What happened to Horace? He was sentenced to death, commuted to life imprisonment and released in 1919. There is a sketch of him in the 30 March 1907 edition of *The Graphic*.

For unequal liaisons resulting in an illegitimate child but no marriage, the father might pay maintenance – though not in the case of William Whiteley! Occasionally, such a father acknowledged a child as his, but because of illegitimacy laws, the child couldn't inherit. Of course illegitimacy occurred in upper echelons of society but understandably was kept discreet.

Bastardy Books
Prior to the 1834 Poor Law amendment, bastardy books for any woman who gave birth to an illegitimate baby were kept in the parish. These state the cost of lying-in plus any allowance paid by the father for his child's subsequent upkeep. Surviving bastardy books are in CROs often on microfilm viewable locally.

The Stockport bastardy book, 1817–30, begins with an address-book style index where babies A/B etc. (e.g. Alexander by Sutton) are listed alongside a number referring to the accounts ledger later in the book. The registers are so discreet that no first names have been disclosed, so a woman with the surname Alexander was made pregnant by a man with the surname Sutton. The accounts state when the bond was set up, dates when monies were paid and how much. Fathers paid mothers between 2s and 3s 6d per week with a one-off lying-in fee (generally around £1 11s). Once a child reached 9 years old, payment ceased. There were other reasons for cessation; the child's death (sadly very common): the father's death: a warrant if he absconded (e.g. Gordon by Hadfield, 25 May 1820): the parents married (Booth by Lee, 28 April 1825): or left the county. In some, 'parents arranged the matter between themselves'.

The Bastardy Clause in the 1834 Poor Law Amendment Act stated that illegitimate children were the sole responsibility of their mothers until they were 16. Evidence of paternity claims were heard at the magistrate's court and it could be difficult to prove a man was the father because it must be 'corroborated in some material particular'. If a mother was unable to support her illegitimate children, she went to the workhouse.

These draconian actions were diluted under 1839 and 1844 Acts, permitting mothers to apply for affiliation orders against a putative father. These, too, were heard in magistrate's courts. Stockport's are dated from 1847. Be warned, records between 1834 and 1844 are difficult to locate because of anomalies in the change in the Poor Laws.

Magistrate Court Records and Bastardy Trials
Magistrate Court Records include bastardy information and may be held either locally or regionally. Stockport's records for 1847 onwards, for instance, are held off site and called up with prior permission from the Magistrate's Court so be prepared to order in advance of a visit. The Magistrate's Court may request a specific date and payment to view records.

Some family history societies publish transcripts of Bastardy Trials. Oxfordshire Black Sheep Publications, for instance, transcribed Oxford City's trials, 1843–1857. *The Miscellany of Bastardy Records* (edited by Jean Cole) for Marlborough and Ramsbury Petty Session Division (1874–84) have been published by Wiltshire Family History Society. Others include Wiltshire 1844–55, and Swindon and District 1869–86. Some societies provide digital versions available to purchase and others have released transcriptions to online

11

subscription services. Publications are listed on the relevant family history websites.

In 1904, in order to reduce the stigma of children born in the workhouse, it was recommended that, when a birth was registered, it should not be recorded as such. Instead, the workhouse address was given, e.g. 123 (later 223) Crescent Road, Crumpsall, rather than 'Manchester Workhouse'. Addresses are found on *www.work houses.org.uk/addresses/index.shtml*. Census records still called it the workhouse. Not all children born in a workhouse were illegitimate. There were a number of other reasons; the 'father's name' column on the birth certificate should offer a clue.

Several workhouse museums are open to the public: Southwell Workhouse, Nottinghamshire *www.nationaltrust.org.uk/the-workhouse -southwell*; Gressenhall Farm and Workhouse, Norfolk, *www. museums.norfolk.gov.uk/gressenhall-farm-and-workhouse*; Weaver Hall in Northwich, Cheshire *http://weaverhall.westcheshire museums. co.uk/visit-us*; Ripon Workhouse Museum and Garden, Yorkshire *http://riponmuseums.co.uk/museums/workhouse_ museum _ gardens*. Other former workhouses have been turned into local museums or converted into apartments. Many, because of their unfortunate reputation and connotation, have been demolished.

Unmarried Mothers' Hostels
The first refuge for unmarried mothers was in Dalston, London, from 1805. Its archives, 1812–1902, are held at Hackney. Until 1848, there was a department for 'male destitutes' but from thereon, the refuge only accommodated women. There were other homes.

In 1836, the London Female Mission opened for servants and 'other unprotected women of good character ... to provide an asylum for fallen, but penitent females'. Wound up in 1881 due to insufficient funds, some of its work had been taken on from 1871 by the Female Mission to the Fallen. Surviving records are catalogued via TNA Discovery, the search engine for The National Archives (TNA) *http://discovery.nationalarchives.gov.uk*, which explains where records are held (locally or at TNA, Kew).

The London Day Servants Hostel provided unmarried mothers with permanent accommodation from 1912. For information about refuges for single women and their children, *www.childrenshomes. org.uk/list/MH7.shtml* and *www.childrens homes.org.uk/list/MH8. shtml* are useful as it lists them, addresses and who was eligible for aid. Homes date from the early 1850s.

Vaccination Certificates

After various smallpox epidemics, the government decided to enforce a vaccination programme. Between 1871 and 1874 birth registrations must include a certificate (overseen by the Medical Officer appointed by the Guardians of the Poor for each area) to prove a child had been vaccinated. Many certificates have not survived, but those that have offer a surprisingly large amount of information. Illegitimate children were inadvertently stigmatised.

Information was recorded in columns similar to a regular birth certificate. Table 1 shows two examples are from microfilmed vaccination records at Stockport Heritage Library.

Table 1. Examples of information on vaccination certificates

	example 1	example 2
when born	7 January 1873	5 February 1873
where born	168 Old Road Heaton Norris	Alegar Fold
name of child	Alfred Burtinshaw	Eliza Burtinshaw
sex	male	female
name and surname of father, mother if illegitimate	Eliza Burtinshaw	Elizabeth Hayes
rank, occupation or profession	–	cotton piecer
date of vaccination	29 January 1873	8 March 1873

to whom given, mother or father	mother	mother
date of medical certificate	7 June 1873	7 April 1873
name of medical man	W Bale	W Bale
date of death if child died before vaccination	–	–

I found two Alfred Burtinshaw/Birtenshaw(s) recorded for Stockport; March 1873 and June 1873. The death of one, aged 0, was registered December 1873.

Abortion
The potential disgrace of being an unmarried mother was so humiliating that women of all classes committed suicide or murdered a new-born baby (Chapter 3). Her third option was abortion.

Following the Ellenborough Act, 1803, abortion was illegal and punishable by death, which was why desperate women attempted to induce a miscarriage instead. Nicholas Culpepper's seventeenth-century *The Complete Herbal and English Physician* (online at *archive.org*) hinted at efficacious herbs but many women knew tansy, penny royal, ergot of rye, savin (from juniper) and antimony (a lead alloy found in cosmetics and bought at a chemist) could produce the desired effect. To countermand this, the 1861 Offences Against the Person Act made self-abortion, procuring or performing one, punishable by life imprisonment rather than a death sentence. Only as recently as 1967 (Abortion Act) was the Act partially amended permitting some stipulated exemptions in England, Wales and Scotland but, at the time of writing, unless complying with those exemptions, the sentence is still theoretically life imprisonment.

The laxative and panacea for everything, Beecham's Pills, went on sale c1842. Under euphemistic advertising campaigns, these treated 'female ailments' to 'promptly remove any obstruction or irregularity of the system' – and swallowed by the handful. Did my tight-laced grandmother realise the other implications when she fed them to me for constipation?

If a new-born child was deformed, sickly, stillborn or died almost immediately, who knew if it were the result of a botched abortion? Unless a passing mention was made in a parish burial register, there were no official records until 1926 when stillbirths had to be registered.

Deaths caused by abortion, and anyone taken to court for attempting to induce an abortion, appear in court records and/or newspapers.

On 11 June 1842, *York Herald* published the case of farmer Thomas Paget and his blacksmith nephew from Hull, William Marshall. They were tried at York Castle for procuring abortion by administering poison to Paget's servant, Elizabeth Richardson who, it was alleged, they forced to drink steel filings. After Paget was accused of being the father, their defence denigrated Elizabeth as 'one of the most worthless wretches through telling falsehoods and general badness of character'. The case was dismissed but not without a suggestion of unease when the judges commented, 'it was a case of great suspicion against them'.

Adoption

Just as shame accompanied women bearing illegitimate children, so it was for those who failed to conceive. This was a potential catastrophe for persons of rank; repercussions involved not just ending a genealogical line but who inherited the family estate. There were medical interventions, none particularly pleasant; Edward Tilt's 1882 gynaecological book cites surgeon Professor James Young Simpson's (1811–70) cure, 'slitting of the womb for the cure of sterility'.

Until the 1926 Adoption Act, adoptions were private, unregistered and informal. A family just took on another child, as happened to my grandfather aged 4 when his father died in 1887.

He merely moved in with an uncle and aunt whilst his mother worked in domestic jobs to support her sister bring up a nephew. Alternatively, children lived with grandparents or neighbours.

There are unlikely to be surviving records apart from the census. If a child was visiting rather than living there permanently, it may be recorded as such. There are no adoption registers or indexes online.

Bibliography

Bull, Thomas, *Hints to Mothers for the Management of Health during the Period of Pregnancy and in the Lying-in-Room*, Longmans, 1877

MacKay, Sinclair, *The Mile End Murder, the Case Conan Doyle Couldn't Solve*, Aurum Press, 2017

McLaughlin, Eve, *A McLaughlin Guide to Illegitimacy*, FFHS, 1989, revised

Paley, Ruth, *My Ancestor was a Bastard: A Family Historian's Guide to Sources for Illegitimacy in England and Wales*, Society of Genealogists, 2004

MARRIAGE

Marry your sons when you will, your daughters when you can
(proverb)

Women were expected to marry. An unmarried daughter was a financial burden on her family and it was unusual for single middle-class women to leave home. On the other hand, plenty of single working-class women were live-in servants whilst others worked as day servants, living at home until marriage. Even after they'd tied the knot, many couples lodged with parents or in-laws for economic reasons.

The average length of a marriage was ten years (death either side) hence why so many married for a second (and third …) time. This practical solution provided a carer for both sets of children plus an income (usually his) to do so. Post 1837, marriage certificates state the condition of bride and groom, i.e. spinster, widow or widower. It's complicated to work out whose children were whose in a census, especially if they assumed the surname of a second husband – similar to the expediency of illegitimate children taking on a step-father's surname. In some cases, both surnames were recorded, with their real father's name taking on the appearance of another Christian name. Today, of course, it might be double-barrelled. Unlike today, there was no official paperwork for this.

Following the 1823 Marriage Act, wedding ceremonies must be held in the parish church between the hours of 8 a.m. and 12 noon, and Sunday and Christmas Day were popular. Why Sunday? The combination of a non-working day and sizeable church attendance ensured a large congregation witnessing the event. Banns were also called on a Sunday. In rural areas where few could read, this provided material proof of a marriage. During the population explosion of the 1850s and 1860s over 40 per cent of London marriages took place on Sunday and large cities countrywide also witnessed this phenomenon. Pity the poor rector, chaplain or curate who officiated for several couples on the same day; Manchester Cathedral celebrated twenty-eight marriages on Sunday 12 April 1857. The following day, Monday 13 April 1857, sixteen couples were married there including my great great grandparents. By the late 1880s, Saturday was superseding Sunday's popularity.

> Marry on Monday for health,
> Tuesday for wealth,
> Wednesday the best day of all,
> Thursday for crosses,
> Friday for losses,
> and Saturday for no luck at all

The folk rhyme is out of kilter with a happy couple's choice of wedding day when Wednesday, Thursday and Friday were, at less than 10 per cent, the least popular. Monday's attractiveness is possibly explained by 'Saint Monday' when self-employed men took an unofficial holiday.

Marriages could be by banns or licence. Banns involved reading aloud the names of the couple in church on three successive Sundays in the parishes of bride and groom (if they lived in the same parish, it was just the one church) so that, should there be an impediment to their marriage (already married, under age, marrying a close relative, etc.) there was the chance of someone informing and preventing it. Plenty of parish church banns plus marriage parish registers survive on microfilm at CROs, local history centres, TNA and online genealogical sites.

For those who didn't wish to have their names read aloud, and there were plenty of reasons (to marry in haste, one or both were well known and wanted to avoid a pre-announced wedding, to avoid potential objections from parents due to e.g. the age of the bride) they could marry by licence for a higher fee. Anyone who married by licence was generally from a higher social class.

Crisp's Marriage Licence Index, 1713–1892, includes abstracts from many original London parish licences. Information in these indices includes couple's names, residence and date of the licence, searchable by year on Ancestry. The condition of the records is poor, especially for earlier dates, and it may take some time to find anything relevant and, should you find a marriage, information is often limited – e.g. the marriage licence for bachelor John Growse to Charlotte Stevens at St Martin's in the Fields, 5 January 1854, gives just that information. The Society of Genealogists *www.sog.org.uk* holds some marriage licence records.

A bond was a formal intention to marry and similar to banns for those marrying by licence. It's not a confirmation the couple actually wed, although it usually incurred a penalty should the prospective groom renege. An explanation of the difference between marriage bonds, allegations and licences for England and Wales is found on the Family Search website (*www.familysearch.org/wiki/en/Marriage_Allegations_Bonds_and_Licences_in_England_and_Wales*). Some marriage bonds issued by the archbishops of York (patchy survival before 1700 and only those up to 1823 are indexed) are at Borthwick Institute for Archives, York University *www.york.ac.uk/borthwick*. Their page at *www.york.ac.uk/media/borthwick/documents/*

5marriage bonds.pdf explains bonds plus an exemplar annotated 1741 bond.

Honeymoons were rare for the working class. Prosperous upper-class couples occasionally embarked on a bridal tour visiting relatives unable to attend their wedding. In France from the 1820s onwards, wealthier couples might take a *voyage à la façon anglaise* (English-style journey).

By the end of the nineteenth century, far more couples managed a few days away after their wedding but, unlike today, left directly after the wedding breakfast following the church service. As described in the *Western Times*, 17 October 1890, Mrs Dorothea Fulford Hawkins née Vicary and new husband Caesar Frederick Hawkins took the 4.12 London train immediately after their North Tawton wedding. Details include a description of the bride's dress, going-away outfit, names of parents and family, groom's occupation, order of service, music and hymns. A hundred guests attended the wedding breakfast at Bouchier's Hill and suppliers of cake, carriages and wedding dress are all identified.

Local, regional and national newspapers are wonderful resources for marriage details of prominent couples and include details like those of Mr and Mrs Hawkins plus notable attendees and occasionally listing wedding presents and who gave what. Less noteworthy people (for this read ordinary couples) also had their wedding in the papers, listing attendees plus relationship to the couple. Be aware that married women were described as e.g. 'Mr and Mrs H. C. Bolingbroke' – the husband's initials, not hers.

For a small charge, births, marriages and death announcements, just names, date and church, were placed in local newspapers. In January 1880 the *Bradford Observer* charged 1s 6d for a maximum twenty-six words and another 6d for each additional nine words.

Newspaper Collections
The British Newspaper Archive (BNA) in association with the British Library is digitising newspapers and can be accessed (subscription) at *www.britishnewspaperarchive.co.uk* or via FindMyPast. Ancestry

subscribers have access to *The Times* (1788–1833), *Gentleman's Magazine Library* (1731–1868) and *The Edinburgh Advertiser* (sporadically, 1771–1909) plus others. Many local libraries hold subscriptions to FindMyPast and/or Ancestry and The Times Digital Archive 1785–1985 (*http://gale.cengage.co.uk/times.aspx*), giving free access to library members. Free access to BNA is with a reader's ticket at the British Library either at St Pancras or at Boston Spa, Yorkshire, see *www.bl.uk/collection-guides/british-newspaper-archive* or *www.bl.uk/reshelp/findhelprestype/news/bna*.

A free newspaper site run by the National Library of Wales is online at *http://newspapers.library.wales* and includes nearly 120 newspapers dating from 1804 to 1910 largely from Wales. The National Library of Australia's newspaper site is also free and contains some articles from outside Australia *https://trove.nla.gov.au/newspaper*.

Photographs

From the 1880s, studio photographs were despatched to friends and relatives. They are much of a style; happy couple plus individual poses wearing everyday clothing, groom in a suit and bride in her best costume perhaps flower as corsage, her left hand prominently displaying the ring. Today's traditional white dress became fashionable following Queen Victoria's marriage (1840) but only took off after the Second World War.

Later, a photograph of new mother and baby was taken and sent to friends and relatives.

Morganatic Marriages

Although there were some infamous exceptions, the aristocracy married within their own class entailing a large dowry or settlement as they did so.

Morganatic relationships, where a man was of a higher social status to the woman, usually did not, because of impropriety, scandal and ostracism, result in marriage. The consequences of such a union are illustrated by the treatment of George Harry Booth Grey, 7th Earl

Wedding photo, Edgar Emm & Kate Masters 1883. Author's collection. © Adèle Emm

of Stamford and Warrington, who married illegitimate circus bare-back rider Catharine Cox at Windsor in September 1855. Shortly after their wedding, they were snubbed by Queen Victoria at the opera and, whilst attending Knutsford Races, had backs and parasols deliberately turned against them. This was his second morganatic marriage! His family had, unsuccessfully, offered a £500 bribe to the daughter of a Cambridge bed and bootmaker when he was 21 and this first marriage lasted until her death six years later. Like many aristocratic families, the Grey family's archives are held privately; in this case at Enville Hall *www.envilleestate.com/enville-estate-archives*. See TNA Discovery for others.

Closer to home as far as royalty was concerned, Prince George, 2nd Duke of Cambridge, clandestinely married a nobody on 8 January 1847. Having failed to get prior permission for his marriage from the reigning monarch (cousin Queen Victoria) under the Royal Marriages Act, 1772 (repealed 26 March 2015), his sons couldn't inherit the title. His wife? Drury Lane actress Sarah Fairbrother (1816–90), daughter of a Westminster servant and mother to a brood of illegitimate children, two of them his.

For men, mistresses were generally condoned. Following his marriage to Sarah Fairbrother, Prince George maintained several, including one Louisa Beauclerk. All three are buried in Kensal Green Cemetery within sixty feet of each other. For those interested in royal liaisons, try Anthony J Camp's website Royal Mistresses and Bastards: Fact and Fiction, 1714–1936 (2007) *www.anthony jcamp.com*.

Once heir and spare had been achieved, aristocratic wives or those in marriages of convenience could largely get on with their own life – as long as she was discreet. There are many examples.

There were rules on who you could marry; we all know you can't marry a sibling or parent but a widower marrying his deceased wife's sister was prohibited in 1835 under Lord Lyndhurst's Act. This not uncontroversial Act spawned several (now obscure) novels where the main plot was exactly that, a man marrying his wife's sister. To name two: *The Inheritance of Evil: Or, the Consequence of Marrying a Deceased Wife's Sister* (1849) by Felicia Skene (1821-1899) and *The Fatal Three* (1888) by M E Braddon (Mary Elizabeth, 1835–1915) whose most famous book is Lady Audley's Secret.

This law was repealed in 1907 under the Marriage to Deceased Wife's Sister Act.

Breach of Promise

A woman was defined by her husband's rank which explains why many women sought economic stability plus status through marriage. An unmarried *spinster* (term derived from a woman who span; *wife* was derived from a woman who wove) was a creature to be pitied. Consider Emma's conduct towards Miss Bates in Jane Austen's eponymous novel and behind-the-back-sniggering (which we've all done) at maiden aunts.

Breach of promise was serious. It compromised a woman's reputation and potential for a second chance at marriage. Before 1875, the case was held in Assize Courts, records are held locally or regionally and notoriously difficult to locate or comprehend. Newspapers containing between-the-lines salacious gossip offer the best bet.

On 28 March 1865, *The Scotsman* reported a case in Manchester's Sherriff Court between Miss Ann Sykes (aged 47, her last-chance-saloon?) and Manager of Manchester Waterworks Corporation, widower Mr T G H Berrey, two-ish years her senior. An excellent catch. The details, addresses, date of engagement, method of proposal and personal correspondence were humiliatingly read aloud in court and reported verbatim in the newspaper. Even an intimate poem, *A May Day Ode*, was printed in full, much, one guesses, to Miss Sykes' mortification. She was awarded £1,250 damages. Four years earlier, in 1861, Thomas G H Berry (sic) was living with wife (coincidentally, also Ann) and son in Prestwich, near Manchester. Five years after the breach of promise trial, spinsters Ann and sister Sarah are living in Worsley on 'interest from money'.

Dowries and Prenuptial Agreements

Originally, a dowry was a portion of land given to a daughter on marriage as an inheritance to be used on her husband's death, hence *dowager*, a widow in receipt of her dowry who lived in the 'dowager's cottage'.

Under the Fines and Recoveries Act, rules concerning a dowry were changed in 1833; a 'fine' was the word for property so a 'fine of lands' was effectively a property conveyance. There was much spiteful newspaper speculation at the engagement of Queen Victoria's second daughter, Princess Alice in 1861. Editorials discussed Lord Palmerston's comment that the country should not send a royal daughter 'forward as paupers', with conjecture on the amount of dowry (recorded as between £40,000 to £30,000 down; and £8,000 to £6,000 per annum) and who should pay it (the country, from taxes paid by the poor or Queen Victoria and Consort Prince Albert).

For poorer women, a dowry chest was often the bottom drawer (the origin of the well-known phrase) where she kept an assortment of household linen, good clothes and underwear to take with her when she married.

Prenuptial agreements had to be signed before marriage. Called *marriage settlements* or *covenants*, they were the only method by which potentially profligate husbands were prevented from snaffling a wife's money on marriage (pre the Married Women's Property Act of 1882, more of this later) and squandering it. Effectively, they were written for women with something worth losing so, unless you have a wealthy heiress in your ancestry, you're unlikely to discover one. A woman's money, perhaps just a portion, and often some of his, were put into trust for her to receive an annual or monthly allowance once married.

This was crucial if he died or was profligate as explained in an initially anonymously published 1863 book, *Guide to the Unprotected in Every-Day Matters Relating to Property and Income* (found free online). The author, banker's daughter Emma Galton (1811–1904), insisted, 'No prudent woman should marry without this provision, as, if it is made before her marriage, however much in debt her husband may become, from extravagance or misfortune, her settlement money cannot be made liable.'

The settlement relied heavily on the Trustee (who could be her husband or relative, always male) but was her money and couldn't officially be subsumed by him.

Other Victorian wives might have small savings accounts opened in their names and banks officially only permitted access to the woman and not her husband.

Surviving settlement records are in CROs and located via their website or TNA Discovery. Information found within them is variable. The following two examples show the difference; the earlier has very little information but the second is a goldmine for a family historian.

First, the 1820 marriage settlement for the Bagot family of Bolton dated 27 December (held at Manchester, ref E3/146) for the intended marriage between William Bagot Esquire of Kingsley and Martha Swinnerton, spinster, of Butterton, both Staffordshire. Detail is merely names, names of trustees and some sparse information on land involved and acreage. It was biased towards the husband with few provisions for Martha.

Sixty years later, in the run-up to the 1882 Married Women's Property Act, one family was greatly concerned about the future of a 22-year-old heiress who, on the death of her father two years earlier, had inherited a fortune. The marriage settlement dated 15 January 1878 (ref E/HULT/22/1, Manchester Archives) for the impending union between William Edward Montagu Hulton-Harrop of Gatton Lodge, Shropshire, to Margaret Henrietta Elizabeth Bewicke of Close House, Wylan on Tyne, Northumberland, is extraordinarily illuminating. Information within this covenant includes:

• full names and addresses
• names of Trustees and addresses
• provisions if left a widow
• all her investments, property owned by her, expected inheritance and value where it was to be invested
• provision for anything she held with bankers, e.g. jewels and trinkets
• provisions if he were profligate
• provision for children, including the event of no surviving child, the birth of one son or only daughters

- provision should she marry after his death and vice versa
- detailed and itemised schedules of his land in acres, roods and perches
- notes recording subsequent death of her husband.

In a nutshell, she was substantially wealthier than her prospective spouse. Both were to invest money into trust for their futures and that of any progeny. She was permitted access to her personal possessions and an allowance free from future interference by her husband. Their marriage bond, St George Hanover Square, is dated 9 January 1878.

A quick check in the 1881 census finds magistrate William, 25, and wife Margaret, also 25, living at Lythwood Hall (now demolished) in Condover near Shrewsbury. Margaret has given him two children, daughter Alyne (born 1878, conceived shortly after the wedding) and the second, coveted first-born son, Hugh (killed in the First World War). Just short of thirty years later, their 1878 marriage settlement was invoked to provide for their children including Alyne and sons Cyril Charles (born 1886) and Victor Edward (born 1889). The young men were awarded an advancement of £1,000 each on 1 December 1909. Their by-now married older sister Alyne Vera Rowan-Robinson waited another three months to receive an annual annuity of £200 in two equal portions per year to commence six months after signing the covenant, 24 February 1910. It ceased at her father's death. This deed of covenant also gave details about her husband, a Captain in the 53rd Shropshire Light Infantry, destined to die in the First World War.

Married Women's Property Acts 1870 and 1882
In 1877 Millicent Garrett Fawcett had her purse stolen at Waterloo Station; the charge-sheet read 'stealing from the person of Millicent Fawcett a purse containing £1 18s 6d the property of Henry Fawcett'. In other words, because Millicent Garrett Fawcett was married, her money and herself were legally her husband's chattels (old French, *chattel*; goods, wealth, possession and cattle).

As aforementioned, women risked losing money and investments on marriage. Even single or widowed women had issues with accessing financial information about investments simply because of endemic patronising and paternalistic attitudes towards them. Emma Galton's 1863 financial *Guide to the Unprotected* (the title itself is self-explanatory) covered topics on marriage settlements, wills, agents' charges, debts, sharing expenses, banks, ground rent, income tax, money orders and telegrams. Today, it appears condescending to a fault but her female contemporaries were dangerously naïve. Galton wrote,

> When you have fixed upon a Banker, and placed some money in his hands, he will give you a book, called a Pass book, or Bank book. The Banker will enter on one side of this book all the money that is paid into the Bank by yourself or by others for you. These sums are called Credits, and that side of the book is called Cr., short for Creditor.

In 1870, following various campaigns by female social reformers, the Married Women's Property Act was passed. This permitted women to keep wages they earned after marriage, inherit property and take court action in their own names. Prior to this, even if a woman received an income from her book sales like socialite Caroline Norton, her estranged husband could – and did – appropriate it. However, he could still do what he liked with her stocks, shares, property etc. – women literally ascribed all money to her husband on their wedding day.

The 1882 Married Women's Property Act went further. It allowed married women to buy, sell, own property and stocks and shares in her own name. Married couples were regarded as two separate entities rather than just one (the husband). On the negative side, she could be sued directly and, because debts were her responsibility not her husband's, she was subject to bankruptcy laws.

However, from here on, married women appeared in electoral rolls. Surviving records and documents are archived locally or regionally, try TNA.

Attitudes towards women and their finances were slow to change. Even in the early twentieth century, they were naïve about financial affairs and in 1903 Lucy Helen Yates (1863–c1935, a journalist working for the *Daily Mail* in 1911) published *The Management of Money; a Handbook of Finance for Women*, offering similar advice and information to Emma Galton half a century earlier. Yates asserted a girl's education must include 'the management of money' and receive a small allowance of £50 to £100 per annum in order to do so. Of course she was writing for the emerging middle class; never in their dreams could the working class afford such sums for a daughter.

For women who owned rateable property in their own names because they were unmarried or widowed, try the Rate Books. These listed people eligible to pay rates for poor law relief and are held locally in CROs or heritage libraries. FindMyPast has some for 1706 to 1900. Ancestry has selected London rate books for 1684–1907. Information revealed is name of occupier, name of owner (if the house was rented this is not the same person), description of property (e.g. land, house, shop), rateable value, how much and when it was collected.

There are also tithe maps of 1848 which show field boundaries plus who owns/leases areas of land. The originals are held at TNA, Kew, although you may find copies in local libraries and CROs, which is where I bought a fabulous coloured facsimile of my area. TheGenealogist and Ancestry have some tithe information online.

Betty Bosson held at least six fields flanking Mauldeth Lane, Heaton Mersey, and is listed on TheGenealogist. Other women holding neighbouring land include Ann Street and Lea Birch but, at a time when women could only hold land if single or widowed, female names are a tiny minority. Betty was buried at St James, Didsbury, on 20 December 1861 aged 75. According to probate records, she died 16 December bequeathing an estate of under £100 to son Thomas, a farmer from Morley, County Chester. You can spot her living alone in Heaton Moor earlier that year mistranscribed in the census as Betty Bossum, widow 'formerly farmer's wife', from Prestbury.

Divorce

A woman badly abused by a husband had pretty little redress; stick it out until one of them died or risk social banishment and perhaps starvation if she left. Taking children with her meant the possibility of them starving too. Without a formal divorce, neither could remarry except bigamously, until one died. Stories abound, not just in fiction but in real life of women forced to remain with brutal husbands. Former schoolteacher Ellen Weeton Stock (1776–c1844) wrote a journal of her life as a governess (1811–25) but other works describe her violent marriage to Aaron Stock, owner of a Wigan factory, who used his wife's pre-marriage money as capital. She left him at least once but had to return. Her journals and letters are at Wigan Archives *https://archives.wigan.gov.uk/archive/the-edward-hall-diary-collection/ellen-weeton* with some digitised pages online.

The 1857 Matrimonial Causes Act was partly the effect of callous and cruel treatment of George Chapple Norton towards his wife Caroline née Sheridan (1808–77). They married in 1827 but following his drinking, possessiveness and violence towards her, she left in 1836, surviving on her earnings as an author of mainly light-weight romantic novels. Because her possessions were legally his, he went to court demanding her earnings should also be turned over to him. Not only did he win, but she was ruthlessly refused access to her children. This appalling set-back forced her to fight back. In 1854, she published *English Laws for Women in the Nineteenth Century* and, because of her influential connections, male ones at that, the following year she was a witness at a government review of the divorce laws.

Before 1857, it was nigh on impossible for a couple to divorce. It required a lengthy, difficult and horribly expensive individual Act of Parliament. Not only this, but, following the divorce, children risked being regarded as illegitimate and unable to inherit. Up to the 1840s, there were about forty divorces a year and a mere 317 in total by 1857.

Because they were Acts of Parliament, records for the pre-1857 divorces are kept at the Parliamentary Archives *www.parliament.uk/*

business/publications/parliamentary-archives (visits by appointment only). A few are in TNA.

The 1857 Matrimonial Causes Act introduced judicial divorce where men could cite adultery and women prove cruelty or desertion. Judicial separation allowed a woman to keep what she earned, gave protection to deserted wives and provision for children's custody. Although divorce was now technically possible for a couple, it was unattainable for ordinary people and its stigma was not something women in particular could face. Some couples claimed non-consummation of marriage (not necessarily true), offering childlessness as evidence.

Records of all divorces since 1858 are held in the Divorce Section of the Principal Registry of the Family Division, First Avenue House, London. There is limited information. TNA has a help-sheet on divorce at *www.nationalarchives.gov.uk/help-with-your-research/research-guides/divorces* giving research options.

Ancestry has divorce files from 1858–1911. Surviving case files from 1858 can be searched by index in TNA J78 (*http://discovery. nationalarchives.gov.uk/details/r/C9686*) and by name in TNA J77 (*http://discovery.nationalarchives.gov.uk/details/ r/C9685*). Case files are destroyed after twenty years.

If a couple could not satisfy the demands of a divorce, their only other option was an annulment or formal separation through church courts.

- Nullity – a marriage was declared invalid from the start. Children automatically declared illegitimate and the wife lost her right to inherit. Reasons were e.g. bigamy, incest or a bride too young to marry. Because this was a church decision, surviving records are locally held.
- Annulment – legal separation where children were regarded as legitimate and wife's rights protected, however neither party could marry again whilst the other was still alive.
- *Jactitation* – no marriage had taken place. In common law, this meant one of the couple said they were married when they

weren't; this action usually precipitated by 'husband' not 'wife'. It's pretty rare but one example, 1820, is when Edward Lord Harley-Hawke threw out Augusta Elizabeth Corri declaring she was his mistress not wife.

• *A mensa et a thora* (divorce from bed and board) – legal separation on grounds of life-threatening cruelty or adultery. The husband may be required to pay maintenance to wife and children.

For records for any of these, try TNA in the first place, especially Close Rolls C54 which also hold records for deeds of separation some of which took place after 1857. Although the Act theoretically made divorce easier, partners were unable to get a divorce because: (1) they held religious beliefs against it: (2) they were incompatible (not a reason for divorce): or (3) they were unable to prove adultery. Occasionally, one of the couple appealed against the decision. First appeals were heard at the Archbishop's Court in Canterbury or York with further appeals at the High Court of Delegates up to 1834, and the judicial committee of the Privy Council between 1834 and 1858. Again, visit TNA website for the location of surviving records which may be held at TNA, Lambeth Palace Library *www.lambethpalace library.org*, or Borthwick Institute of Historical Research *www.york. ac.uk/borthwick*.

A famous deed of separation was obtained in 1858 by Charles Dickens against wife Catherine Thomson Hogarth (1815–79), mother to his ten children. Following the then law, all the children who lived with their father at Gad's Hill Place, Kent (apart from eldest son Charley, 21, above the age of majority) were discouraged from visiting her. If she never attempted to contact him, she received £600 annual maintenance. He couldn't file for divorce because she'd never committed adultery, but still he persisted in discrediting her any manner he could, including wrongly accusing her of alcoholism. They were not divorced so neither could remarry. In his will, he left £1,000 to actress Ellen Ternan, £8,000 to his sister-in-law Georgina Hogarth and the same sum to his sons with the proviso they helped their mother. Catherine survived him by more than a decade.

A more everyday example of what can be discovered from divorce records (in this case via Ancestry) is that of Agnes Anne Smith who petitioned for divorce from husband Ernest Albert in February 1894; final decree 6 May 1895. They had married very young, merely five years earlier; he 23, an auctioneer living at Kilburn Priory, she 18. The church register records his father, Alpheus, as 'a gentleman' and hers a schoolmaster but the 1891 census reveals Ernest's father as nouveau riche accountant from Ilkeston, Derbyshire, former coal and iron merchant.

In 1891, a year after their marriage, they are an obviously well-to-do family. Ernest, Agnes, daughter Nora, Agnes' mother Jane Ford and a nephew lived together at 1 Derby Villas, Grove Vale, Camberwell. Ernest is an auctioneer/estate agent and his mother-in-law of independent means.

The divorce records include:

- petitioner's name and address
- wife's maiden name
- solicitors' names and addresses
- reason for divorce; adultery, cruelty, threat and physical abuse; paperwork includes names plus dates of alleged infidelity; reasons for divorce petition and examples (often upsetting)
- access to children; names and birthdates
- monetary issues – e.g. how much to be paid to the petitioner
- petitioner's costs and who pays
- date and place of original marriage
- matrimonial address
- Respondent's reply to accusations and reciprocal allegations.

After the divorce, Agnes married Edward Valentine Low (the witness!) in September 1895 and in 1901 was living with him and her mother in Edmonton. Her children were elsewhere.

Contemporary newspapers published the juicy details – everyone enjoys a scandal.

Bigamy

When divorce was economically or feasibly impossible for the average couple, the only available recourse (apart from celibacy) was live in sin or marry bigamously but bigamy was a risky venture. If caught, consequences were harsh.

Bigamy literally means 'having two wives'. However, other terms were used including *polygamy*, a man having more than one wife, and *polyandry*, a woman having more than one husband. From 1603, the punishment for being caught in a polygamous relationship was death although by the early nineteenth century usually commuted to transportation. Under the Offences Against the Person Act (1861) the sentence was reduced to branding one hand plus seven years transportation or two years imprisonment.

If there's no record of the death of a spouse but another marriage, this may be the reason and wasn't particularly unusual in the nineteenth century especially amongst the working class. If a couple moved away, who was to know about a previous spouse?

A common motive for condoned bigamy was when a spouse was presumed dead as depicted in Thomas Hardy's *Far from the Madding Crowd* (1874) following the assumed drowning of Sergeant Troy. In my family, it was transportation. No one expected to see them again. Did they survive the voyage? Did they survive life in the convict camp? They were as good as dead and under common law, could be declared dead *in absentia* after seven years.

Scattered throughout family histories around the 1830s and 1840s (including mine) are tales of babies born several months after a husband had been transported – an alternative version to posthumous birth.

The February following his arrest and imprisonment for rioting and machine wrecking in December 1830, James Case was transported for seven years to Van Diemen's Land (Tasmania). He left behind wife Ann Case née Moxam plus five children to be supported on the parish. A few months later, Ann gave birth to a son who could just have been conceived before James was imprisoned and transported. However, James couldn't have been

33

responsible for the birth of William Blick Case in December 1836. In 1841, George Blick, Ann's lodger, is presumably keeping the family off the parish and in 1849, the two marry. As James Case was very much alive in Van Diemen's Land, this marriage is theoretically bigamous but who was to know? Transportation records state James was illiterate and more than eighteen years had passed. After so many years of cohabitation, their Wiltshire vicar must have been relieved to finally marry them.

Pity the plight of Agnes Breslin/Fish, reported in the *Edinburgh Evening News*, 19 October 1898. In 1885, she married a man called Fish, and walked out after four children and four years of violent marriage. Nine years later, November 1897, hearing (unreliably) that Fish was dead, she married a miner named Mc'Allister with whom she had another child. Unfortunately, it was Fish's sister who'd died and Agnes was imprisoned for bigamy.

Others believed (or wanted to believe) that, if a couple were separated for over seven years, they were free to marry. This happened, as reported in the *Bath Chronicle and Weekly Gazette*, 7 November 1895, to Mary Easton who married carter William Holbrook, 57, knowing he was already married but had been separated for over seven years. William was sent to prison for one day then discharged. Some hot-shot defence!

No one admits to bigamy but don't jump to the conclusion that a marriage was bigamous just because you can't find a death, annulment or divorce. Police records, assizes, and Old Bailey reports plus newspapers might unmask a guilty ancestor. Newspapers reported bigamy cases including the sentence. Social commentators Henry Mayhew and Charles Booth mention the subject in passing.

Bibliography and Further Reading

Chapman, Colin R, with Litton, Pauline M, *Marriage Laws, Rites, Records and Customs, Was Your Ancestor Really Married?*, Lochin, 1997

Frost, Ginger, *Living in Sin: Cohabiting as Husband and Wife in Nineteenth-Century England*, Manchester University Press, 2008

Galton, Emma, *Guide to the Unprotected in Every-Day Matters Relating to Property and Income* 1863, free online incl. later editions

www.historyofwomen.org/marriage.html

Jalland, Pat, *Women, Marriage and Politics, 1860–1914*, Oxford University Press, 1986

Norton, Caroline, *English Laws for Women in the 19th Century*, Privately publ., 1854

Stone, Lawrence, *Broken Lives: Separation and Divorce in England, 1660–1857*, Oxford University Press, 1993

Yates, Lucy Helen, *The Management of Money: A Handbook of Finance for Women*, Horace Cox, 1903

DEATH

As already explained, childbirth was a major cause of maternal death in Victorian and early twentieth-century England and Wales. If a woman dies young or disappears from records, the likelihood is she died in childbirth and this was regularly recorded on death certificates. With the lack of feasible and reliable contraception, women commonly had more than ten children in quick succession, each birth increasing the odds of something going wrong during labour. It wasn't just the strain of giving birth, there was also the major threat of puerperal fever. In 1911, death from this was estimated at two per thousand.

Puerperal pyrexia or puerperal fever (a form of septicaemia) was a hazard caused by unsterilized instruments or other lacks in hygiene. Seemingly healthy women developed a high fever a few days after giving birth and subsequently died. Isabella Beeton fell victim in 1865, aged 28, following the birth of her fourth child. Other terms found on death certificates for this terrible infection were post-partum sepsis, childbed fever or womb fever.

My great grandfather's first wife, Rebecca Harris née Winwright, died in 1880 giving birth to her first child. Attending her, as was common, was her mother-in-law who registered the death. The certificate states, 'Effusion on brain, 1 hour, puerperal convulsions,

REGISTRATION DISTRICT					NEWPORT PAGNELL UNION			
1880	DEATH in the Sub-district of Newport Pagnell					in the County of Buckingham		
Columns:– 1	2	3	4	5	6	7	8	9
No.	When and where died	Name and surname	Sex	Age	Occupation	Cause of death	Signature, description and residence of informant	When registered	Signature of registrar
97	Twenty Second December 1880 Poggs Court	Rebecca Harris	female	26 years	Wife of Thomas Harris Soda Water Maker Labourer	Effusion in Brain 1 hour Puerperal Convulsions. 3 hours Certified by C Terry m R C S	S Harris Mother in law present at the death Mill Street Newport Pagnell	Twenty Second December 1880	Jno Paine Registrar

Rebecca Harris death certificate, 22 December 1880, pre-eclampsia. GRO

3 hours.' Today, we know this as pre-eclampsia, a term in existence from at least the 1860s, still potentially fatal. It was also recorded on death certificates as toxaemia.

Another fatal threat was haemorrhage. There were three main causes. Before the birth, a woman bled to death if the placenta separated from the womb early or during childbirth. Alternatively, if the placenta blocked the birth canal (placenta praevia), baby could not be born and if surgical intervention caused internal damage mum risked massive blood loss, or died from infection. Today, women receive an emergency or elective caesarean; high-risk before the twentieth century. Thirdly, should the afterbirth not come away once baby had been delivered, mother faced unstoppable bleeding.

Because of the cost, doctors were rarely called to childbirth unless a problem arose; by then, it was often too late. Even eminent doctors (Sir Richard Croft for instance) preferred not to intervene and left it to mother nature; a laissez-faire strategy with potentially tragic consequences.

Just as now, other causes of death were female complaints (e.g. breast and uterine cancer) but, because of the lack of modern technical expertise and antibiotics, what killed women between 1815 and 1914 might not be a death sentence today.

								HC 770762

CERTIFIED COPY of an   ENTRY OF DEATH
Pursuant to the Births and   Deaths Registration Act 1953

Registration District Newport Pagnell

1900 . Death in the Sub-district of Newport Pagnell   in the County of Buckingston

Columns: -	1	2	3	4	5	6	7	8	9
No.	When and where died	Name and surname	Sex	Age	Occupation	Cause of death	Signature, description, and residence of informant	When registered	Signature of registrar
122	Thirteenth October 1900 13 Mill Street U.3.	Elizabeth Harris	Female	72 Years	Widow of John Harris a Labourer	Uterine Cancer 1 Year Certified by H.T. Wickham M.D	A Harris Daughter-in-law Present at the death 13 Mill Street Newport Pagnell	Fifteenth October 1900	Geo H. Simpson Registrar.

Elizabeth Harris death certificate. Uterine cancer, 1900. GRO

Cancers were recognised but only 2 per cent of deaths in the nineteenth century were from this disease. According to her death certificate, my great grandmother died of uterine cancer. Other terms were malignancy, tumour, carcinoma or growth, perhaps with the affected part of the anatomy cited. The first radical mastectomy (although performed in France a century earlier) was achieved in 1882 in America by surgeon William Halsted.

Edward Tilt in his 1882 book *Women at the Decline of Life* espoused various therapies for the menopause. Among the least disagreeable were bleeding (leeches behind the ear), an hour-long warm bath at about 93° two or three times a week tempered by a stream of cold water to the head and stomach, or 'the sudden shock of sea bathing'. More extreme remedies included (today locked in the poisons cabinet) alkalis, sulphur, borax, strychnine, arsenic, antimony or ammonia – all administered to alleviate hot sweats, dyspepsia and constipation or diarrhoea depending on symptoms. The cure was more dangerous than the complaint.

This is not the place to list common ailments but following the big killer childbirth, was phthisis, consumption and TB – all terms for types of tuberculosis. Although this disease was not a female monopoly, twentieth-century research by Andrew Hinde of the University of Southampton (2011) suggested that, if a woman lived in poor rural areas like southern England and East Anglia, a 5-year-old girl was more likely to die from TB three years earlier than her twin brother. Why? Because her brother, working as an agricultural labourer, brought in a wage and, consequently received more and better quality food. The pulmonary diseases, tuberculosis, pneumonia, asthma, bronchitis, pleurisy etc. carried people off in their thousands, including the Brontës, Elizabeth Barrett Browning (died 1861), and Elizabeth Siddal, the model who posed for Ophelia 'drowning' in Pre-Raphaelite artist John Everett Millais' eponymous painting. The cold bath was arguably responsible for her death, in 1862, aged 32.

Consumption was seen as a glamorous death in Victorian literature, art, theatre and society. I only need to name the following, *Jane Eyre* (1847), *La Traviata* (1853), Elizabeth Gaskell's *North and South* (1854), *Les Contes d'Hoffman* (1881) and *La Bohème* (1896), all of which have a tubercular female victim central to the story. Victims of the disease slowly wasted away and the consumption-chic aesthetics of thinness, pale skin with blue veins showing through, pink cheeks, rosy lips and silky hair were described in Arnold Carl Klebs' 1909 treatise on TB.

You may see 'visitation from God' in records. This was when a doctor had no idea what killed their patient. It may have been a euphemism for starvation but don't regard it thus in every case. However, should a cause of death be 'want of the necessities of life', yes, this probably was starvation.

Before the welfare state, dying of starvation was a real possibility. On 6 September 1864, the *Western Times* wrote of London's 'shame and sorrow' where in 'the richest city in the world' Miss Lucretia Jefferies from a formerly prosperous family died 'the agonies of slow starvation'. The details are heart-rending; 'When the Coroner's Jury went to the lodgings of the family to view her body, they found no furniture there but a box, a broken chair and a parish bed, upon which the elder sister lay.' She and her sister had tried to earn a living sewing shirts for a slop-seller near Bedford Square but, falling sick with overwork, neither they nor their parents earned 'a farthing' for eight weeks. The family had progressively sold their possessions, and, once reduced to penury could not face the final ignominy of the workhouse. The journalist concluded, 'It is no doubt true that the family might have applied for admission to the workhouse, though recent painful experiences induces us to feel not absolutely certain that they would have been received.' The Civil Registration Death Index records Lucretia Jeffery (sic) dying in Mile End, December quarter 1864 (1c 443).

The death of 21-year-old Mary Smith was reported in *Shields Daily Gazette and Telegraph*, 28 October 1881. No feckless wastrel or ne'er do-well but a Keighley mill hand who, with her out-of-work brother, was caring for three younger orphaned siblings. Had brother and sister sacrificed themselves for the younger ones?

Regional dialects have different terms for starvation. In Lancashire, it was 'clemming' to death.

When somebody died, the sexton tolled the bell for about 1s a toll, once for a child, twice for a woman and three times for a man – reconfirming his superior status. For those who belonged to a burial club, it covered the funeral fees but for those without the wherewithal, the parish paid for a pauper burial, a payment increasingly resented post the 1834 Poor Law hence why so few after this date. Some registers of pauper burials exist, for instance those between 1861 and 1868 for Newton Heath, Manchester, but information is minimal; name of deceased, place of residence, burial date, age at burial (weeks and months for infants; years for adults) and who performed the ceremony.

Ann Fidler, 69, from the Manchester Workhouse, received a pauper burial on 15 January 1868. In the 1861 census, two widow washerwomen, Ann Fidler and relative Sarah Ratcliffe, lived in Back Hardman Street (possibly a back-to-back, see Chapter 4). In hindsight, it's easy to understand why they ended up (a) in the workhouse and (b) paupers' graves. They were widowed with an occupation of final resort and desperation – washerwoman (see Chapter 5).

If your ancestor was in the workhouse when she died, you can guarantee she had a pauper's burial. It was common for several pauper funerals to be performed the same day and in 1860s Newton Heath, the person conducting the majority was Rector William Hutchinson. Paupers' graves were dug deep, often up to eighteen bodies interred together (adults, children and babies) in one unmarked plot. Generally, coffins were not separated by soil unless the deceased had perished from a contagious disease when slaked lime was poured on top. The grave was closed when full.

Some Manchester (1800–1911), Westminster and Cheshire workhouse death and burial records are on FindMyPast. Ancestry holds some London workhouse burial registers. Family Search (free) has Cheshire and Norfolk workhouses. Other surviving records (e.g. Newton Heath as above) are held in the CRO. Some councils and archives have burial records online such as Manchester City Council's free index on *www.burialrecords.manchester.gov.uk*. Records for Tameside's Dukinfield Cemetery is at *http://web. tameside.gov.uk/ BACAS*.

Holding records mainly from the 1850s, *www.deceasedonline.com* has a free index but you must pay for detail. The National Burial Index is on FindMyPast.

Coroner's bills
Some local history societies have transcribed coroner's bills. Wiltshire, for instance, published *Transcriptions of Wiltshire County Coroner's Bills, 1796–1823* in 2012. Unexpected deaths were investigated with comments like 'suddenly expiring in her bed' or 'sudden death' (e.g. Hester King of Preshute, 26 June 1817). Fits were common. More poignant are the reminders of the stigma of illegitimacy. Mary Clements of Avebury 'Died from the effects of taking poison to procure abortion', 27 May 1817. To find what is available, check FHS websites.

Wills and probate

Wills and probate were for those who had something to leave so, before 1882 and the Married Woman's Property Act, only widows and single women were likely to make them. Spinster Eleanor Sophia Harrison died 8 February 1860 leaving a healthy estate worth nearly £2,000 to Granville Diggle Hill, a solicitor. Her address on the National Probate Calendar was 'formerly of Hereford but late of 3 Laura Place, Bath'. A quick check of the 1851 census finds her, aged 32, living there, the residence of Granville D Hill, solicitor. She is enumerated as sister-in-law and 'householder'.

Her brother-in-law Granville Diggle Hill died 3 May 1888 also at 3 Laura Place, bequeathing his entire estate of £8,270 16s 6d to his 'widow, the Relict and sole Executrix' Susannah Hill née Harrison, Eleanor's sister. Because Susanna had married before 1882, she could not have directly inherited her sister Eleanor's estate.

Relict, as inscribed on gravestones, monuments and in probate is from Latin *relictus*, 'having inherited' or 'bequeathed', and is, theoretically, a woman who has survived the death of her husband for several years. She is not, therefore, a recently widowed woman.

Before the Court of Probate Act 1857, which came into force January 1858, wills and probate were proved by ecclesiastic courts. The National Probate Calendar for 1858–1996 is available on the GRO website *https://probatesearch.service.gov.uk/#wills*. The type of information found includes:

- name and date of death of deceased and date of probate
- where they originate, possibly an address; where they died, which could be in hospital
- state, e.g. widow, spinster, and occupation
- effects, e.g. under £20, under £100, under £20,000
- name of beneficiary and relationship, e.g. son, daughter, executor/executrix (a female executor)

Ancestry holds probate records from 1384 (Prerogative Court of Canterbury Wills) plus others. Women are predictably under-represented. If you want a copy of a will dating from 1858 you must apply online at *www.gov.uk/search-will-probate* with the date of death. At the time of writing, copies cost £10 each. There are different procedures for Scotland *http://webarchive.nrscotland.gov.uk* and Northern Ireland *www.nidirect.gov.uk/proni*.

Surviving hospital records compiled by the Wellcome Trust are held at TNA *www.nationalarchives.gov.uk/hospitalrecords*.

HOSPREC (Hospital Records Database) is not, at the time of writing, included in Discovery. Records, because of confidentiality, are closed for up to 100 years.

The Voluntary Hospitals Database at *www.hospitalsdatabase. lshtm.ac.uk* includes an explanation of voluntary hospitals, i.e. before the NHS was established in 1948. An online map shows the location of voluntary hospitals and clicking on the name links to more information plus where archives might be held. Nottingham Hospital for Women, for instance, was founded 1875 as Castle Gate Hospital for Women (1875–c1893) in Castle Gate, Nottingham. Records (listed) are held at Nottingham University Library.

Bibliography and Further Reading
Death, wills and probate

Annal, David, and Collins, Audrey, *Birth, Marriage and Death Records: A Guide for Family Historians*, Pen & Sword, 2012

Baines, M A, *Excessive Infant Mortality, How Can it be Stayed?* Paper contributed to the National Science Association, 1862/1868

Hewitt, William Morse Graily MD, *The Diagnosis and Treatment of Diseases of Women, Including the Diagnosis of Pregnancy*, London, 1863

Hodges, Richard, *On the Nature, Pathology and Treatment of Puerperal Convulsions*, London, 1864

Jalland, Pat, and Hooper, John, *Women from Birth to Death: The Female Life Cycle in Britain 1930–1914*, Humanities Press, 1986

Kellogg, J H, *The Home Hand-Book of Domestic Hygiene and Rational Medicine*, volumes 1 and 2. Oakland, CA, Kellogg, 1881

Klebs, Arnold Carl, *Tuberculosis: A Treatise by American Authors on its Etiology, Pathology, Frequency, Semeiology, Diagnosis, Prognosis, Prevention, and Treatment*, Appleton, 1909, *https://archive.org/details/tuberculosistrea00klebuoft*

Leared, Arthur, *Infant Mortality and its Causes*, reprinted from *English Woman's Journal*, 1862

Raymond, Stuart A, *The Wills of Our Ancestors: A Guide for Family and Local Historians*, Pen & Sword, 2012

Taylor, Nigel, and Grannum, Karen, *Wills and Probate Records: A Guide for Family Historians*, The National Archives, 2009

Tilt, Edward John, *The Change of Life in Health and Disease: Women at the Decline of Life*, J. & A. Churchill, 1882

Wills, Simon, *How Our Ancestors Died*, Pen & Sword, 2013

General further reading

Edwards, John William, and Hamilton, William Frederick, LLD, *The Law of Husband and Wife with Separate Chapters upon Marriage Settlements and the Married Women's Property Act 1882*, Butterworths, 1883

www.forebears.co.uk useful overview for locating resources, websites and databases including online parish clerks, many free

Fowler, Simon, *The Workhouse: The People, the Places, the Life Behind Doors*, The National Archives, 2007; Pen & Sword, 2014

Foyster, Elizabeth, *Marital Violence: An English Family History, 1660–1857*, Cambridge University Press, 2005

Steinbach, Susie, *Women in England 1760–1914: A Social History*, W&N, 2005

Symes, Ruth A, *Unearthing Family Tree Mysteries*, Pen & Sword, 2016

Chapter 2

EDUCATION

In an affluent family, the sons' education received priority so why would a manual labourer educate his daughter?

When education cost money, even only a few pennies a week, few working-class parents laid out hard earned cash to teach a child to read and write when they must pay rent, feed and clothe a family. In the countryside, girls worked the land, weeding, hoeing, keeping chickens, milking cows, raking, binding, stoking cereals at harvest to earn perhaps a penny a day, far less than brother and fathers earned, but essential income. In towns and cities, girls worked in factories. Women didn't need to read or write.

As large families were the norm, working-class daughters helped with housework and minded younger siblings, especially when mum was in the family way, nursing baby or, as was regrettably so common, dead. Girls' education was low priority apart from practical activities, needlework (making and mending clothing), housework (including laundry), basic cooking on the range (ovens in many cottages were unheard of) all taught by her mother.

Even in the early twentieth century, a girl's extensive education was discouraged; it distracted her from tending husband and nurturing his children. Literature in the guise of novels was inappropriate; books by George Eliot were anathema – a novel about unmarried mothers written by an unmarried woman openly cohabiting with a married man, nothing could be more scandalous! Certain passages of the Bible were 'racy' and might distress a woman's sensibilities. No wonder fashionable girls' schools concentrated on innocuous subjects like music, French, deportment, drawing (flowers not life-studies), the globe (capital cities) and handwriting.

The Birmingham Statistical Society on behalf of the Royal Commission on Employment of Children estimated (1838) that less than 50 per cent of children received any education between 1821 and 1831. By 1838, the number of children receiving no education at all (girls constituted the larger proportion) was estimated at: Westminster 66 per cent, Liverpool 53 per cent, York 38 per cent, Manchester 31 per cent and Bury 18 per cent. These statistics prove that Northern industrial cotton cities Manchester and Bury were educating children, albeit in factories or Sunday School. By the 1860s, one-third of children did not attend school in any guise whatsoever.

Even a basic signature was low priority. In the mid-nineteenth century, 45 per cent of women couldn't even write their name, signing a marriage register with their mark (usually x). Only 31 per cent of men were illiterate enough to do this.

So what opportunities were there for girls to gain an education? Some local industries combined rudimentary literacy skills with teaching girls e.g. to make lace.

Schools for girls as young as 5 were established in Bedfordshire and Buckinghamshire, especially around Olney. The heyday was the first half of the nineteenth century. Girls learnt to make bobbin lace and, depending on the school, basic reading and writing, but, most importantly, earned 6d for a six to seven hour day.

Records for lacemaking schools are sketchy and held locally. The Cowper and Newton Museum in Olney *www.cowperandnewton museum.org.uk* has examples of lace, a webpage on its history including fabulous photographs of women making lace. Olney boasts a designated lace walk around the village, and the Olney and District Historical Society has a series of lacemaking articles by Liz Knight and links to parish registers and buildings *www.mkheritage. org.uk/odhs*.

MILLS

The workplace occasionally offered an opportunity for education. Before the 1819 Cotton Mills and Factory Act, there was no legal minimum age to work in factories. Scavengers as young as 5 collected combustible fibres from beneath dangerous spinning machines. From 1819, the law banned children under 9 although, as there was insufficient enforcement, many factories simply ignored the law. Those who complied might provide educational opportunities not only for their child workforce but for adult employees' children too.

In 1786 Jedediah Strutt (1726–97) opened his first mill in Belper, Derbyshire, insisting millworkers' children were educated on Sundays in a room at the top of the mill. Radically for those days, they were taught elementary reading, writing and arithmetic. By 1818, the Strutt family had built Long Row School (still in existence although rebuilt) catering for both girls and boys.

Belper Mill Infants School (1881–3) and Belper Mill Girls Day School Wages and Admission Register (1819–24) are held at Derbyshire Record Office with a copy at Belper Library. A volunteer run website, *www.belper-research.com* explains background and local personalities, and links to census and parish records, although some are subscription based.

Textile mills employed young children on apprenticeships. These offered an employer a cheap stable workforce by legally enforcing a child from the age of 7 (legislation increasingly raised the age) to work for a set number of years without pay whilst the employer trained, housed, fed and clothed them. Parents or guardians signed (or put their mark) on the indenture and a child was contracted to work for up to seven years; in some mills, considerably longer. After 1833, it became compulsory for mills to give apprentices a basic education (not all employers complied) – the more socially responsible were already doing so.

The Apprentice House at Quarry Bank Mill (*www.nationaltrust. org.uk/quarry-bank*) accommodated its apprentices from 1790 to 1847. Aged upwards from 9, there were twice as many girls as boys.

As many were orphans unsure of their birthday, height was used to determine age.

The owners of Quarry Bank, the Greg family, prided themselves on their social conscience, and paid apprentices overtime at the rate of 1d an hour. Potentially this accrued to make a welcome nest egg for a girl once her apprenticeship was complete, although apprentices were punitively fined for transgressions such as lateness, swearing, bad behaviour or breaking windows.

Importantly, three nights a week after a thirteen-hour shift, girls were sent to the schoolroom. Here, they concentrated on learning needlework and housekeeping but also, taught by Mrs Greg herself, received a smattering of literacy.

Apprentice house, Quarry Bank Mill, National Trust. The school room was on the ground floor. © Adèle Emm

Anyone with ancestors working at Quarry Bank Mill, Cheshire, is fortunate indeed. The mill is unique in that, because all records survive, names of apprentices and employees are known together with pay, fines for infractions, and medical records. At the time of writing, they are unavailable to the general public but there are plans to put them online (see *www.nationaltrust.org.uk/quarry-bank/ features/explore-the-archive-of-quarry-bank*). There is a myriad of books about Quarry Bank, including David Hanson's *Children of the Mill*, which accompanied Channel 4's television drama *The Mill*.

For more on apprenticeships and working in mills, see Chapter 5.

THE PART-TIME SYSTEM/HALF-TIMERS

Following the 1833 Factory Act, it was compulsory for mills to provide children under 13 with two hours of elementary schooling a day. This led to a half-time system where, theoretically, children simultaneously earned a wage and education, effectively continuing into the early 1920s. Under this, half-timers worked from 6.30 a.m. until 12.30 with school from 2 p.m. until 4.30. The following week, times were reversed, school in the morning from 9 a.m. until 12 noon and factory work from 1.30 p.m. until 6.

Four male inspectors, Leonard Horner, T Jones Howell, Robert J Saunders and James Stuart, were appointed to enforce this Act reporting to the government in *Returns*. They had the power to demand a certificate proving a child had attended school for a certain number of hours a week but, with so many factories and only four inspectors, it was a challenging task. In each *Report on the Effects of the Educational Provision of the Factories Act* (e.g. 1837, 1838), they explained findings, naming factories and in some cases children attending school, parents, mill owners, and transgressions, such as no surgeon's certificates or children working after hours on Saturdays and subsequent fines imposed. Some e.g. *Parliamentary Papers, House of Commons and Command*, vol. 50 (1837) are found online via Google Books. In an 1838 report, a register of children aged under 13 includes Mary, Jane and John Weir who attended Mill School, Garlogie, Aberdeen, for two hours every day (excluding

Saturday) on the week ending 2 September. Owned by Messrs Alexander Haddon and Sons, the forty or so children at the worsted mill were taught reading, writing, geography, English grammar and accounts by teacher William Mitchell, each receiving a certificate on Monday morning. Factory Inspector Reports are held either at TNA or locally; check Discovery for what is available.

SUNDAY SCHOOLS

The Sunday School movement was founded in Gloucester in 1780 by Robert Raikes (1736–1811) to teach children to read the Bible. For those working full-time during the week, this was their only opportunity to receive an education. By 1831, over one and a quarter million children, a quarter of the juvenile population, were taught at Sunday School. Run by religious groups, churches and Nonconformist chapels (largely Baptists and Methodists) they met on Sunday when factories were closed. In mid-nineteenth-century Birmingham, fifty-six Sunday Schools catered for 16,757 scholars, their attendance averaging at just under 73 per cent. Only twenty-five schools taught writing; slates were expensive . . .

Because Sunday Schools were attached to religious institutions, the curriculum generally followed the church's teachings although it also depended on the staff's principles and skills. As Sunday was a day of contemplation, many activities were deemed unsuitable for the Sabbath. Girls were taught sewing.

Most Sunday Schools divided genders into a girls' and boys' division. Supplementary benefits were provided, including clothing clubs especially for girls often with a donation at Christmas. What a godsend for a poor family. There were other welcome treats such as processions and parties for Whitsuntide (the Whit Walks) and coronations (e.g. William IV in 1831), and summer picnics where benefactors donated cakes and fancy food.

Neither Sunday Schools nor associated clothing clubs were necessarily free; a charge of 1d a week was normal but anyone too poor to pay was exempt. Fundraising was common and popular schemes included Sunday sermons delivered by the local vicar where

St Matthews Sunday School, Liverpool Road, Manchester, built 1827. © Adèle Emm

Detail St Matthews Sunday School, 1827. © Adèle Emm

girls sang psalms and hymns – the collection was allocated to that specific school. Such events were reported in local newspapers (e.g. Ansty Girls' Sunday School in *Leicester Journal*, 25 September 1835) although references to specific children are uncommon.

*Thurston Newton, superintendent of girls Sunday School, Ashton Under Lyne.
Are they dressed for the Whit Walks? Author's collection © Adèle Emm*

Records are held in CROs. Try TNA Discovery to track them down but they often consist merely of minutes, annual reports and accounts. Some parish magazines from the 1860s survive and may name prize winners.

One of the largest Sunday Schools in the world was in Stockport and its Heritage Library *www.stockport.gov.uk/heritage-library-archives* holds an important collection of records, 1793–1963, including registers, minutes, financial records and correspondence.

WORKHOUSES
Under the 1834 Poor Law Act, Poor Law Unions (the Union Workhouse) had to provide a rudimentary education for children

under its jurisdiction; three hours of education per day for girls and boys. A schoolmaster or mistress was appointed to teach them.

Girls, taught in a separate schoolroom, covered the predictable syllabus: sewing, household management (girls cleaned the workhouse rather than someone else being employed) and bare essentials of reading, writing, and arithmetic. As academic study was not a priority, many girls didn't learn to write. By not buying slates or styluses, Unions saved money, as was the case in Bedford, 1836. It also perhaps explains the low percentage of women able to sign their name on marriage.

Timetables were prescriptive. In Marylebone Workhouse School in the 1840s, girls rose at 6 a.m. to make beds, clean shoes, wash, pray and take religious instruction. Breakfast and recreation was between 8 and 9 a.m., followed by reading, spelling, tables and arithmetic, writing in copybooks and dictation until lunch at 12.30 – the designated three hours of education as prescribed in the Poor Law Act. Dinner and recreation was until 2 p.m. when girls were set to knit, sew and perform domestic duties until the evening meal and further recreation at 5 p.m. for an hour. Evenings were spent in needlework, knitting and domestic employment until bedtime at 8.

A useful explanation of the history of the workhouse and their schools can be found at *www.workhouse.org.uk* created by Peter Higginbotham and its sister site *http://childrenshomes.org.uk* providing information about children's homes and orphanages.

Workhouse records and archives are generally in CROs. Subscription genealogical sites such as FindMyPast and Ancestry feature workhouse admission and discharge records.

BRITISH AND NATIONAL SCHOOLS: MONITORIAL SCHOOLS

The British and Foreign School Society was founded 1808 and schools set up under its aegis were effectively monitorial schools largely run by religious organisations, Nonconformist or Church of England.

Monitorial schools were essentially the brainchild of Scottish

Minister Andrew Bell (1753–1832) and Joseph Lancaster (1778–1838) who believed huge numbers of poor children could be taught in one room – over 100 children was not unusual. Older and brighter children became monitors working around the edge of the classroom. Indeed, Lancaster's first school, Borough Road, London, with Lancaster as sole adult teacher, had over 500 pupils. Rote learning was the modus operandi for reading, writing and arithmetic – the three Rs – and because girls' education was a low priority, they had a lower pupil–teacher ratio. For an 1814 address by Ann Springmann about monitorial schools for girls see the US website *www.constitution.org/lanc/mon4girls.htm.*

With so few teachers, such schools were cheap to implement and maintain, and their popularity grew rapidly – for educationalists and funding authorities if not parents. By the 1840s the monitorial system was in place virtually everywhere, both church and parish schools. A few national schools erected in the 1830s and 1840s still exist, typically located near the church after which they were named. Such schools were generally day schools so it's hard to discover which school an ancestor attended although, as they often survived the 1870 Education Act, records, year books and alumni lists for instance, may exist online at e.g. Ancestry and FindMyPast.

CHURCH SCHOOLS AND PARISH SCHOOLS
Like the National Schools, these were also voluntary – parents paid to send their children. A large proportion of teaching was based on the tenets of the church's beliefs and, when the monitorial system was popular, taught pupils by this method.

Some church schools were charity schools. Burlington School (founded for Promoting Christian Knowledge in Carnaby Street, London, 1699) is the fourth oldest charity school for girls in England. Its original intention was to teach 'sixty poor girls (whose parents could not afford them education) to read, write and cost accounts . . . and instructing them knowledge of the Christian Religion'.

Initially a day school, it was funded by charity sermons and annual subscription from patrons. By 1725, after the construction of a new building, girls aged 10 to 15 were boarded, clothed and fed. When they left, they were put into service or apprenticeship (this ceased by the mid-nineteenth century). By 1842, recreation consisted of walks in nearby parks; in 1848 girls bathed every Saturday night. That year, their diet was ratified (as decreed by Bell and Lancaster of monitorial school fame) with bread and milk for breakfast (a treat of rice milk on Sundays) and a rotation of boiled beef or mutton, suet pudding and soup for midday dinner, bread and butter or cheese in the evening. They were allowed beer and water to drink. When they left for their first position, they were given:

• a new gamblet gown and a house gown
• two petticoats, one white, one coarse
• three check aprons
• two pairs of shoes and two pairs of stockings
• three shifts and four caps
• a Prayer Book and Nelson's Festivals and Fasts

After a year's service in the job, they received:

• a Bible
• Slade's Exposition of the Psalms
• Levi's Exposition of the Church Catechism (found free online)

By 1861, Burlington took in paying scholars and, briefly, boys under 8. Its curriculum had expanded to include French, natural sciences and 'body exercise', similar, perhaps, to fictional Pinkerton's School for Young Ladies as depicted in Thackeray's 1848 novel, *Vanity Fair*. The school's name was changed in 1876 to Burlington Middle Class School.

The 1851 census lists Miss Jessie Rowlatt (enumerated as Rowlett) as matron and servant in charge of Burlington School, Boyle Street, St James; her sister Emma (governess), plus staff (cook, assistant, housemaid) and girls ranging in age from 10 to 15. As there are no surviving admission records for the school at this time, this is the

Burlington Girls' School uniform from 1810. By courtesy of Burlington Danes Academy, West London.

only record of the 1851 scholars and it's interesting to note that they, as in the original school policy, were local, from Middlesex. By 1861, girls came from a wider catchment area including Lancashire, Gloucester, Cambridge and Oxfordshire and boarded from the tender age of 6.

By 1876, following the 1870 Education Act, the school was brought into the London School Board system; trustees were replaced by a board of twelve governors but it continued with its liberal education of the 1860s. Fees were charged at £1 10s or £1 5s per term according to age; school hours were 9.30 to 12.30 and 2 to 4 in the afternoon. It had reverted to a day school.

The school still exists, albeit a coeducational academy Burlington Danes in White City, Shepherd's Bush. The Wellcome Institute holds some medical records (1848–1972) *http://wellcomelibrary. org/moh/report/b19956356/128#?c=0&m=0&s=0&cv=128* whilst the Hammersmith and Fulham Archives and Local History Centre hold some twentieth-century minutes, correspondence and papers. See TNA. Records post-1940 are at the school and subject to data protection.

RAGGED SCHOOLS

All schools apart from charity schools, workhouses and apprentice houses charged fees so there were millions of children who either had no inclination or couldn't afford to go.

In the first half of the nineteenth century, social reformers were appalled by the poverty and child crime they saw around them, especially in the cities. Charles Dickens depicted *Want* (female) and *Ignorance* (male) as children in *A Christmas Carol*, 1843.

One of the earliest Ragged Schools, opened 1842 in London's Field Lane, was visited by Charles Dickens in 1846, and his letter describing it in the *Daily News* can be read at *www.infed.org/archives/e-texts/dickens_ragged_schools.htm*. The British Library page *www.bl.uk/romantics-and-victorians/articles/ragged-schools* gives further information on both school and his visit.

In 1844, Anthony Ashley Cooper, 7th Earl of Shaftesbury, established the Ragged School Union with an initial core of nineteen schools countrywide. Open during the day for dirty, unkempt and unruly children (many were homeless, others had been in prison), to access rudimentary education, they were volunteer run, free and often provided food, clothes and lodging, although these, depending on circumstances, were at minimum charge. Pretty soon, some opened two or more evenings a week, providing an education for adults working during the day and apprentices such as shoemakers.

The children's behaviour was described as wild, especially that of those attending London's Strand school set up 1863 by baronet's son and ex-Etonian, Quintin Hogg (1845–1903). One of his sisters

Entrance to Working Girls' Home, part of Charter Street Ragged School, Manchester. The girls' school was upstairs.© Adèle Emm

was persuaded to run a girls' class with a reputation as challenging as their brothers'. Hogg's Ragged School ultimately became London Polytechnic, now University of Westminster.

By 1870, there were over 250 ragged schools in London and 100 plus elsewhere teaching basic reading, writing and counting.

The Ragged School and Working Girls Home on the corner of Little Nelson Street and Dantzic Street in the shadow of Angel

Meadows (one of the most notorious and impoverished areas of Manchester) was founded in 1844. Based above the Charter Street Ragged School (boys) on the ground floor, girls were taught homemaking and cookery. Clogs, clothing and food were also supplied. Charter Street Ragged School's archives 1857–1996 include deeds, minutes, reports, financial records, registers, correspondence, photographs and sole miscellaneous papers held at Greater Manchester CRO (ref; GB124–5), who also hold archives for Openshaw Sunday Ragged School (1883–1975) and others.

However, the Ragged School Union Annual Report for 1857 revealed that, out of an estimated half a million children living in London, only 21,500 attended lessons or used their services and that, of the 563 children registered at the Field Lane School, only 275 attended regularly.

A letter written by the Inspector of Reform Schools published alongside a speech given by Unitarian Minister's daughter Mary Carpenter (1807–77) in Coventry, November 1861, highlighted the problem. 'It cannot get hold of the children who won't come to it themselves, and it cannot retain those who are themselves willing, but where parents will not let them attend, and withdraw them – usually for vicious purposes – from its shelter.'

For background information on ragged schools, it's worth grazing local newspapers at the BNA. Ragged schools' records are locally kept and depend entirely on what has survived. Take Stockport Heritage Library for instance. They hold a cornucopia of material for the Ragged School and Industrial Schools 1854–1959 and photographs c1865. Frozen in time, this treasure trove names many girls and staff members including Alice Holt, Edith Adshead, Louisa Ross, Elizabeth Davis and Mary Ingham. They lived in the home based in Hillgate, Stockport, and Louisa Ross, for instance, is there in 1871, born Stockport, aged 10. For the online Stockport Image Archive ragged school photographs see *http://old.stockport.gov.uk/sia*.

TNA lists local records such as Warrington Ragged School, 1899–1943 (Warrington Library and Museum Services). Stonefield's Ragged School accounts, Bilston (1866–1907), are in Wolverhampton (ref; DX/473/1). There may be little individual genealogical information in such records and many are boys' schools. Some ragged schools published magazines but survival is sketchy and they were often published as fundraising material.

The Ragged School Museum in Tower Hamlets, London, *www.raggedschoolmuseum.org.uk* is on the site of Dr Barnardo's Copperfield Road Ragged School. It doesn't hold historical records. Any in existence are at the London Metropolitan Archives. Dr Barnardo's archives *www.barnardos.org.uk* dating from the 1870s are accessed via their Family History Service and there are charges. At the time of writing, it costs an initial non-refundable fee of £15 to check the name of an ancestor against their records.

SCHOOLS OF INDUSTRY/INDUSTRIAL SCHOOLS

Originally, these were voluntary with parents paying for children to learn a skill, the first opening in Kendal in 1799. Younger girls were taught knitting but her elder sisters learned sewing, lacemaking, spinning, house and laundry work whilst preparing breakfast supplied to scholars at an extra weekly charge. Staff constituted a schoolmaster and shoemaking instructor for boys; two women taught the girls.

Having already established Kingswood Industrial School for boys in Bristol, Unitarian Minister's daughter, Mary Carpenter opened the country's first girls' reformatory at Red Lodge, Park Row, Clifton, 1854. Accepting up to fifty-two girls referred by courts after sentences of five years' or less imprisonment, her aim was to educate them for meaningful and honest lives instead of a criminal future. Red Lodge's regulations are at *www.childrenshomes.org.uk/Bristol RedLodgeRfy/BristolRedLodgeRfyRules1854.shtml*.

Her retraining system caught on. The Industrial Schools Act was passed in 1857 when magistrates could despatch homeless, vagrant or begging children who appeared to be aged between 6 and 14 to an industrial school where they boarded and learned a trade protected from deleterious influences. As always, the premise was if a child had a trade, the parish was later spared their upkeep.

For girls, the trade was laundry work, domestic service and ubiquitous needlework/seamstressing. Parents were expected to contribute towards her keep but so many children were homeless, fees were nigh-on impossible to collect. Children wore uniforms; for girls a utilitarian smock, military style for boys.

From 1870, Industrial Schools were the responsibility of the Committee of Education. By 1891, girls received her minimum three hours academic instruction a day with a smattering of geography, history and music. She undertook needlework, laundry, cookery and housework but hours were limited to between four and six a day. On Sunday, they attended church or chapel although parents could object to a particular denomination. Two hours were set aside for recreation.

Admission and discharge dates were recorded by the superintendent, often with comments on the child's behaviour.

Matron/Superintendent's Reports highlight social conditions of the day and sound remarkably familiar; surviving Matron/Superintendent's Reports are extremely illuminating. As many Industrial Schools were boarding schools, pupils, described as 'inmates' or 'scholars', are found in the census so if you can locate the relevant report, you may find references to your ancestor.

Stockport's Girls Ragged and Industrial School founded 1888 at Churchgate, Stockport, relocated, 1890, to 67 Dialstone Lane, Offerton (now an hotel). In 1901, its 'students' hailed from Leeds, Sheffield, Leicester, Gravesend, Cumbria, London, and Wales, plus nearer by.

Miss Janet Wotherspoon, matron from its foundation to closure, wrote a report (held at the Heritage Library) every month from 1890 to 1922 addressed to the Committee governing the school. Many of her concerns were surprisingly familiar. In 1893 she wrote, 'Miss King, the sewing mistress, who was appointed three months ago, has left. She was quite unable to manage or control the girls and was doing more harm than good in the school.'

Other details are heart-rending. The 5 November 1913 entry mentions Lilian Price (or Prince) 'dangerously ill' from tonsillitis

Stockport Industrial School for Girls, now a hotel. The original building can be seen behind the hotel façade. © Adèle Emm

pharyngitis. Gwendoline and Florence Hughes from Caernarvon, aged 9 and 11, were admitted from 'a wretched home and had been much neglected'. On a lighter note, the girls celebrated Guy Fawkes night with venison, parkin and treacle toffee.

There were several reasons for admittance, not purely a criminal record. Being 'uncontrollable' was one but not all girls were wrongdoers; some were admitted through neglect like poor little 'Catherine Milliard aged five and four months sent by the Society of Prevention of Cruelty to Children as being under improper guardianship – found wandering and begging', as recorded in Stockport, 21 November 1894. In 1901, she's in the census as Bolton-born Catherine Hillier. Rescuing Catherine worked; in 1911, Catherine Hilliard (sic) is a domestic servant working at Oxford Road Station, Manchester.

From the age of 14 (more commonly 15), girls might be sent out to work 'on licence'. If they misbehaved, they were immediately returned to the Industrial School. Criminal acts resulted in being handed over to the police. Surviving licences are found in CROs and include the following (not necessarily all) information.

- name
- date they left the school
- age at leaving – years and months (e.g. 15 9/12)
- school register number
- name of employer
- address of employer
- occupation of employer
- capacity in which the child will be employed, e.g. servant, shop assistant
- remuneration, e.g. 3s a week
- other allowances – e.g. bed, board and washing (their clothes) when wages are increased – e.g. according to ability, at end of twelve months
- amount of increase, e.g. 1s, according to ability
- where child will reside, e.g. with people taking them on
- standard passed on leaving school, e.g. 6th standard, 3rd standard, 4th standard, 7th standard
- particulars of outfit supplied to the child: if girl is supplied with clothing, and how much it cost.

Some girls' reformatories together with reasons for admission, daily routine and meals are listed on Gerald Lodge's website at *www. manchester-family-history-research.co.uk/new_page_2.htm.* Another website dedicated to children's homes is *www.childrenshomes.org.uk/ IS/index.shtml.*

Advertisements for staff were published in newspapers. Advertising in *The Scotsman* October 1904, a licenced schoolmistress was paid between £55 and £60 per annum with board and lodging included. In September 1913, giving her a glowing reference from

Stockport, the matron mentions Miss Cross, assistant teacher for the past three years, taking up the post of school mistress at Hull Girls' Industrial School at a salary of £60 per annum.

Records for Industrial Schools are kept locally in CROs.

ELEMENTARY EDUCATION ACT 1870

It took the 1870 Elementary Education Act to change the face of working-class education. From the mid-1800s, there had been a huge demand for clerks – always men. However, the 1870 Act made school attendance compulsory for all children aged 5 to 13. Suddenly, girls were included in the education system potentially learning more than sewing, knitting and housework skills, although these remained an important part of the curriculum.

It was initially relatively simple for parents to avoid sending girls to school. First, it wasn't free, although theoretically those in poverty had fees paid for them. Stockport, for instance, charged ½d a day even for half-timers who were resented by teachers. Because such children spent half a day in the mill, they were behind in their education and consequently fared worse in examinations. Paid by result, teachers' salaries were reduced and therefore they were disinclined to chase up absentees.

It was a financial blow for hard-up parents to lose a child's income or home help with younger siblings and there was little official inducement or enforcement. Only when the law was changed in 1891 was school attendance finally free for all.

Private schools still existed for those who could afford to pay or disliked daughters mixing with the hoi polloi.

BOARD SCHOOLS

Instigated under the 1870 Education Act, these provided schools in areas where there were insufficient places for working-class children. Board schools were administered by locally elected bodies with women now able to vote for and be elected onto school boards (Chapter 6). The boards received funding from the local rates but, unlike voluntary church schools, religious teaching was non-denominational. Any child listed in the census as 'scholar' after 1870 may have been attending a board school.

For areas with sufficient schools, church and national schools for instance, they didn't needed to provide any more under the Act, and existing schools remained largely unchanged. Stockport was one such area.

Girls and boys were generally taught separately. Although many Victorian and Edwardian schools have been demolished, a few stone lintels above doorways bear witness to girls' and boys' separation at the front door. They had separate playgrounds, some existing into the 1960s. Girls might be taught different subjects on a different floor to her brothers. Even in small village schools where children were taught in the same classroom, genders were on opposite sides of the room with windows so high, scholars' attention couldn't wander – still apparent in old school buildings.

The school bell rang at 9 a.m. pealing out from a tower. Lunch (called dinner) was at 12 noon and lasted two hours. No meals were provided; some brought their own but the majority went home hence the two hour break. School usually finished at 5 p.m.

The Education (Provision of Meals) Act of 1906 introduced free school meals for poor scholars, breakfast (commonly porridge and bread) and dinner (lunch). The nutritious meal was provided on a budget of 1d per child supplied free to poor children who ate after those well-to-do enough to go home or bring something in. Because this Act made the provision of school meals voluntary, it was not taken up everywhere.

By 1890, some larger urban schools provided facilities for domestic science for girls and gymnastics, art and craft for everyone.

Attainment expectation was low. To receive exemption from schooling and permission to work, different boards expected different levels; a boy or girl in Birmingham needed only achieve Level IV (Standards of Education contained in the Revised Code of Regulations, 1872) which meant children had to

Originally founded as a National School, the girls' school moved in 1880 to Elm Grove, Didsbury, Manchester. © Adèle Emm

- read a few lines of poetry or prose at the choice of the inspector
- write a sentence slowly dictated once, by a few words at a time, from a reading book, such as is used in the first class in the school
- in arithmetic know the compound rules of common weights and measures

In Bolton, however, she had to achieve top Level VI which required her to:

- read with fluency and expression
- write a short theme or letter or an easy paraphrase
- calculate proportions and fractions (vulgar and decimal)

Given that 45 per cent of girls made their mark with an x less than fifty years earlier, this was an ambitious target when school attendance was not yet compulsory.

It did become compulsory under the 1880 Education Act; and now employers were forced to prove workers under 13 had a certificate of educational attainment.

Existing records for board schools are held locally. You might be lucky and find admission registers; for instance, Hollis Temporary Board School (1874–96), held at Rotherham Archives and Local Studies. But now many board and national school admission registers from 1870 have been digitised and can be found online via subscription services.

Ancestry holds admission registers for London schools 1840–1911 for over a million students in 843 schools. An example: Selina Maude Emm (my fifth cousin once removed), date of birth 6 October 1878, was admitted to Sleaford Street School, Wandsworth, 25 August 1884, a board school opened 1874. She was 5. A year later, she transferred to New Road School, Wandsworth Road (also opened 1874, rebuilt 1927). In 1890, aged 11, she attended St Peter's School, Lambeth (opened c1881, closed 1980) on 29 September 1890. Presumably she left aged 13 as permitted by law. Her father's name is recorded in the registers.

FindMyPast has admission and log registers for national schools from 1870 to 1914 with all schools listed in alphabetical county order at *www.findmypast.co.uk/articles/britain-national-school-admission-registers-and-log-books-school-list.*

Depending on data collected when the records were compiled, you might learn a scholar's date of birth, name of school, admission date, child's address, parent's name (usually father's) and occasionally his occupation.

UPPER- AND MIDDLE-CLASS EDUCATION
Governesses
Giving a daughter an academic education was, for many wealthy parents, irrelevant. It was her accomplishments which counted. As

sardonically depicted by Jane Austen, these were the means to an end – an acceptable marriage to an eligible moneyed husband. Charlotte Brontë scandalised her reading public by having Jane Eyre, an outspoken, plain (but educated) woman catch a landed gentleman.

Well-to-do girls were largely educated at home with a governess (or succession of governesses), specialist tutors for piano, dancing and drawing, and sent to a small boarding school, often abroad, for 'finishing'. Why governesses? They were cheaper than sending a girl to school.

The life of a governess was difficult. Living in a shadowy world, she was subject to the whims of resentful girls who saw her as a poor creature but mutually ignored by servants, her social inferiors. Most were genteel, poorly educated distressed gentlewomen; a large proportion were clergymen's daughters (Anne Brontë's Agnes Grey was semi-autobiographical) and they earned about 20 guineas a year (£21) inclusive of board and lodging.

In her 1868 pamphlet, *The Education and Employment of Women*, social reformer Josephine Butler (1828–1906), best known for her work with prostitutes, wrote;

> In 1861 there were 80,017 female teachers in England, of whom the majority were governesses in private families. It is difficult to ascertain the average salary of governesses, because the Governesses' Institutions in London and Manchester, which are the chief sources of information on the subject, refuse to register the applications of governesses who accept salaries less than £25 a year. The number of this lowest class may be guessed from the fact that for a situation as nursery governess, with a salary of £20 a year, advertised in a newspaper, there were five hundred applicants; as I have already stated, three hundred applied for a similar place with no salary at all.

Why would women work as a governess for no pay? Quite simply, it provided her with somewhere to live where meals were provided.

The alternative was inconceivable. The maximum any governess asked (only ten in the above report did so) was £60 or more per annum. To put this into perspective, male schoolteachers often earned more than £100 a year, more than the headmistress of their school.

In 1829, to alleviate the plight of impoverished former and currently employed governesses as cited by Josephine Butler, a Governesses Mutual Assurance Society was formed. Some archives for 1843–1979 are held at the LMA, including minutes for the Board of Management 1843–1979 and the secretary's letter books 1846–9. There are other records; search Discovery at TNA.

What a girl learned at home depended on the governess' knowledge and expertise. French was considered useful, as were drawing, music (especially playing the piano), sewing, reading and writing, the globe, deportment and etiquette. That was often it!

Small girls plied needles stitching samplers presenting an inspirational phrase from the Bible (or sententious proverb) to marry sewing skills with knowledge of the alphabet. As her anticipated future was to run a household via servants, she required knowledge of basic book-keeping (perhaps) – but cook made meals, servants prepared fires, made beds and did the washing and cleaning. Nanny and governess supervised the children.

Schools for wealthy girls were small and careful not to upset fee-payers – the parents – by being overly academic.

Boarding Schools

There was a wide range of establishments. Some were brutal, a fictional example being Jane Eyre's Lowood based on the Brontë sisters' unhappy experience at the Clergy Daughters' School, Cowan Bridge, Lancashire.

On the other side of the literary coin was Miss Pinkerton's Academy for young ladies on Chiswick Mall (Thackeray's *Vanity Fair*). The school was a 'stately old brick house' where, after six years, a girl was proficient at music, dancing, orthography (hand writing), needlework and embroidery, geography, deportment (continued post-school using the 'backboard for four hours daily for the next four years'), religion and morality. Girls' boarding schools cost about 120 to 130 guineas a year (£126–£126.50) plus extras for dancing, Italian, drawing, etc. Compare this to a governess at £20 a year or free . . .

For a girl with a hankering for an academic in-depth education, it must have been frustrating. It was certainly insufficient for Frances Mary Buss and Dorothea Beale, both pioneers of academic education for girls and who demanded more than needlework, deportment and dancing.

Day Schools

Artist's daughter Frances Buss (1827–94) was sent to a succession of private girls' schools, teaching by 14. She was one of the earliest students attending evening classes at Queen's College, Harley Street, founded 1848 by Professor Frederick Denison Maurice (1805–72) initially to train teachers.

This was the first institution in the world awarding academic qualifications to women. Charging fees of £22 to £28 a year (although there were scholarships) plus extras it was not for the impecunious. Renamed North London Collegiate School for Ladies (NLCS), it moved premises to Camden Street in 1850 with Miss Buss, who coined the term 'headmistress', as head. By 1865, this private school accommodated 200 day girls and a handful of boarders. In 1870, following the Education Act, Miss Buss handed the reins to the Trustees and in 1871 started up a more affordable school, Camden School for Girls.

Another influential educationalist was surgeon's daughter Dorothea Beale (1831–1906), governess-taught followed by schools in Stratford, Essex, and Paris. Alongside Frances Buss, she was another early Queen's College student and, gifted in mathematics, appointed a tutor there in 1849, headmistress in 1854.

In 1858, Miss Beale became Principal of Cheltenham Ladies College (*www.cheltladiescollege.org*), a girls' school opened four years earlier at a cost of £2,000 and with eighty-two day-school students.

By 1863, there were 126 girls, rising to over 1,200 in 1912 with more than a hundred teachers.

At last, girls' academic education (for the prosperous) was taken seriously although only by a minority. It was a challenge attracting parents to part with money for a daughter's education and a fine line balancing accomplishments with academic subjects. Even charging as little as £15–£19 per annum, many were unable to attract and retain pupils. Girls' schools in Newton Abbot and Weymouth, for instance, were out of business by c1895.

Miss Beale, in a preface to the 1869 commissioners' *Reports on the Education of Girls*, complained about poor teaching in most girls' schools and commenced training teachers, (Chapter 6). Stigmatised as 'blue stockings', dedicated to girls' education and disinclined to lose their intellectual freedom, neither Misses Buss nor Beale married. Both NLCS and Camden School for Girls still exist; Camden is an all-girls comprehensive school admitting boys in the sixth form and NLCS is an independent school. Archives for these, like many others (e.g. Manchester High School for Girls, dating back to 1874 and alma mater of the Pankhurst sisters *www.mhsg archive.org*), are held at the school. NLCS archives, dating from its 1851 foundation are held in the McLauchlan Library on the school premises, Edgware *http://library.nlcs.org.uk/archive.html*. For Cheltenham Ladies College contact the archivist at the school *www.cheltladies college.org/about-clc/history-of-college/archives*. At the time of writing, there is a fee of £10 for information although for parents, pupils and Guild members (alumnae), the service is free. Their website *www.cheltladiescollege.org/about-clc/history-of-college/college-in-one-hundred-objects* displays 100 school artefacts dating back to its foundation.

The Society of Genealogists *www.sog.org.uk* has a large collection of school records on the top floor of its library, admittedly the majority for boys' public schools (many dating back centuries). However, amongst its school histories are e.g. Norwich and Blackheath High girls' schools. The SoG library also has a selection of admission registers, for instance, for Preston (1795–1822),

Caverswall (1811–33) and Oulton Abbey (1853–1969). Information includes, if known, dates of birth, confirmation (for a Catholic school) death, marriage, parentage and relationships. The records for Oulton Abbey are more comprehensive. The SoG only have what has been donated or acquired so check their catalogue before trekking a long way to get there.

The Foundling Museum *http://foundlingmuseum.org.uk*, based at Coram Fields, was established 1739 by Thomas Coram to care for abandoned babies, boys and girls. Children were taught skills and trades; girls to run a household or work as a servant. From its inception in 1739 until the last child was placed in foster care (1954), it has cared for and educated over 25,000 children. Its extensive records are held at the LMA and the catalogue is at *http://search. lma.gov.uk/scripts/mwimain.dll/144/LMA_OPAC/web_detail/REFD+A~ 2FFH?SESSIONSEARCH*.

A website dedicated to English education devised by Derek Gillard is found at *www.educationengland.org.uk/history/chapter01. html* and you may also like to taste Richard John's blogspot at *http://richardjohnbr.blogspot.co.uk/2011/02/educating-girls-1800-1870-revised.html*. An overview of the Victorian education system written by the British Library is at *https://www.bl.uk/victorian-britain/articles/ education-in-victorian-britain*.

Contemporary newspapers give a flavour of school life, especially trips and picnics but naming children is rare.

Bibliography

Ardern Burgess, Marion, *A History of Burlington School*, Burlington School, 1949

Barnes, Samantha F, *Manchester Board Schools 1870–1902*, the Victorian Society with Alan Baxter Foundation, 2010

Beale, Dorothea, *On the Education of Girls, A paper read at the Social Science Congress, October 1865, and reprinted from the Transactions*, Bell & Daldy, 1866

Beale, Dorothea, *History of Cheltenham Ladies College, 1853–1904*, Cheltenham Ladies College, 1904

Binfield, Clyde, *Belmont's Portias: Victorian Nonconformists and Middle-Class Education for Girls*, Dr William's Trust, c1981

Brandon, Ruth, *Other People's Daughters: The Life and Times of the Governess*, Orion, 2008

Brontë, Anne, *Agnes Grey*, (novel), 1847

Burchell, Doris, *Miss Buss' Second School*, Camden School for Girls, 1971

Burstall, Sara A, *Frances Mary Buss, an Educational Pioneer*, SPCK, 1938

Butler, Josephine, *The Education and Employment of Women*, Liverpool, 1868

Cobbe, Frances Power, *The Life of Frances Power Cobbe* [an associate of Mary Carpenter at Red Lodge Reformatory School, Bristol], Swan Sonnenschein, 1904, online at *https://archive.org/details/lifefrancespowe02atkigoog*

Davies, Emily, *Higher Education of Women*, Bloomsbury, 1866, online at *https://archive.org/details/highereducation00davigoog*

Digby, Anne, 'New Schools for the Middle Class Girl', in Peter Searby (ed.), *Educating the Victorian Middle Class*, History of Education Society of Great Britain, 1982

Gear, Gillian Carol, 'Industrial Schools in England, 1857–1933: "Moral Hospitals" or "Oppressive Institutions"' PhD thesis for University of London, 1999 *http://eprints.ioe.ac.uk/6627/7/DX211996_Redacted.pdf*

Hodgson, W B, *The Education of Girls and the Employment of Women of the Upper Classes*, Two lectures, 2nd edn, Trubner, 1869

Hughes, Kathryn, *The Victorian Governess*, Hambledon Continuum, 2001

Hunt, Felicity, *Gender and Policy in English Education, Schooling for Girls 1902–1944*, Harvester Wheatsheaf, 1991

Hunt, Felicity, ed., *Lessons for Life: the Schooling of Girls and Women 1850–1950*, Oxford University Press, 1987

Kamm, Josephine, *How Different from Us, A Biography of Miss Buss and Miss Beale*, J Lane, 1958

Lancaster, Joseph, *The Lancasterian System of Education with Improvements*, Baltimore, 1821, *https://archive.org/details/lancasteriansys00instgoog*

Montague, C J, *Sixty Years in Waifdom: The Ragged School Movement in English History*, Woburn Press, 1969

North London Collegiate School 1850–1950: A Hundred Years of Girls' Education: Essays in Honour of the Centenary of the Frances Mary Buss Foundation, Oxford University Press, 1950

Parkes, Bessie Rayner, *Remarks on the Education of Girls, with Reference to the Social, Legal, and Industrial Position of Women in the Present Day*, Chapman, 1854

Raikes, Elizabeth, *Dorothea Beale of Cheltenham*, Archibald Constable & Co., 1908

Renton, Alice, *Tyrant or Victim? A History of the British Governess*, Weidenfeld & Nicolson, 1991

Ridley, Annie E, *Frances Mary Buss and her Work for Education, etc*, Longmans, 1895

Robinson, Jane, *Bluestockings: The Remarkable Story of the First Women to Fight for an Education*, Penguin, 2010

Sewell, Elizabeth Missing, *The Principles of Girls Education*, 1865, and *Amy Herbert*, (novel), 1844

Steadman, F Cicely, *In the Days of Miss Beale: A Study of her Work and Influence*, Burrow, 1931

Turner, Barry, *Equality for Some: The Story of Girls' Education*, Ward Lock, 1974

Wotherspoon, Janet, *Matron's Reports of Stockport Ragged and Industrial Schools*, Stockport Heritage Library, 1888–1922.

Chapter 3

CRIME AND PUNISHMENT

On the whole, we women are a law-abiding lot compared to men and the past was no different. Scroll through petty sessions magistrates registers, for instance, and discover a mere one or two women per page generally for misdemeanours including: failing to buy a railway ticket, non-payment of the Poor Rate (in 1880, one woman was called to court for a debt of £2 19s 3d, was she a suffragist?), importuning, drunken and riotous behaviour. A handful were 'in breach of the Education Act', presumably failing to send their children or part-timers to school (Chapter 2).

More upsetting are female plaintiffs taking a husband to court for assault or applying for maintenance after separation. Others appealed for bastardy payments – these were complainants not transgressors.

Criminal records are less common in more prosperous households although they do appear. Higher courts reveal darker, more serious crimes.

Modern sensibilities mean many of us are amused, even proud of our black sheep: a hawker convicted for no licence; convicts populating Van Diemen's Land at the beginning of the nineteenth century. Most of us can understand and possibly forgive prostitution if it's a matter of survival for a woman and her children. Far less palatable are baby farmers, infanticides and back-street abortionists.

PROSTITUTION
If you seek the oldest profession in the census, you'll be disappointed. Enumerators cavilled at recording a woman as such.

At my estimate, using TheGenealogist website, only 180 prostitutes were recorded for the entire 1841 census in England and Wales, the majority held in a police cell, prison, house of correction, lock hospital for venereal disease, workhouse or 'lunatic asylum'. Few prostitutes were enumerated as such within the community yet, just three years later, Frenchman Léon Faucher exposed Manchester's seedy side with 500–600 'more decent prostitutes' congregating outside the Royal Exchange where business men traded cotton, 'the rendezvous of the wealthier classes'.

Of course there were more prostitutes than revealed in the censuses. Glasgow missionary William Logan published *An Exposure of Female Prostitution in London, Leeds and Rochdale, and Especially in the City of Glasgow* in 1843, explaining the plight of the many prostitutes he encountered during his mission. For many, prostitution, even part-time, kept them from starvation.

Daniel Kirwan's 1870 travelogue *Palace or Hovel or Phases of London Life* (see *https://archive.org/details/palaceandhovelo00 kirwgoog*) reveals police estimated 'a startling aggregate of eighty thousand unfortunates' plying their trade in London. Another police figure, 1867, calculated 24,999 in England and Wales, 5,628 in London. Even though these numbers don't tally, they're considerably higher than revealed in the census – a mere sixteen brothel-keepers in 1871.

Where were the prostitutes if enumerators were reluctant to expose the trade? They were recorded by the last (or any) prior occupation; servant, laundress, shop assistant, etc. In 1890, Revd G P Merrick, chaplain of Millbank Prison, suggested 90 per cent of Millbank prostitutes were daughters of unskilled working-class men and servants, laundresses, barwomen, costermongers and charwomen.

Some online forums infer seamstress and shop assistant were euphemisms for fallen women. However, if you find a shop assistant or seamstress in a census, check where she lived; don't raise an eyebrow at the daughter of a respectable suburban high street grocer. Suspicions are one thing but unless she's convicted of prostitution, don't jump to this conclusion. Take comfort from Sir Charles Warren, London's Police Commissioner in the 1870s–1880s, who, fielding complaints about male harassment by women in the King's Cross area stated, 'The Commissioner doesn't think the police are justified in calling any woman a common prostitute unless she so describes herself or has been convicted as such . . .'

Some areas in London and industrial cities were notorious. The anonymously authored *A Swell's Night Guide through the Metropolis*, 1841, is an early example of what today would be called a listings magazine. Only five copies of this book survive worldwide, one in the British Library Rare Books department. Describing a brothel as a 'house of accommodation' or 'French House' (other Victorian synonyms are *third class house* and *house of ill fame*) he suggested where to find them including (then as now, expensive salubrious areas): Jermyn Street, Cleveland Row, Bury Street, St James Place, Piccadilly, Somerset Street, Hereford Street, Connaught Terrace, Seymour Street, Berkeley Street, York Street, Baker Street and Regent Street.

Was this book the source of subsequent vilification of an entire trade? One example is 'Madame Dentiche, Bury Street, St James' who 'conceals the nature of her calling by carrying on the business of milliner and dressmaker'. I checked the 1841 census. Three dressmakers, E. Dentiche, aged 30, Celine Dentiche, 25, and another female Dentiche, 50, resided together in Bury Street, St James (HO107/736/4/22/38). He also cited Madame Dobeoille at 5 Somerset Street. Such women, hiding in plain view, masqueraded as milliners, dressmakers and servants.

For anyone suspicious of a female ancestor in Westminster in 1841, it may be worth consulting *A Swell's Night Guide* to check if she's there. The second half of this handy guide lists 'Paphian Beauties', a scurrilous and libellous list of London's notable courtesans. For those who had 'fallen' into the profession, the writer recounts her sexual history (occasionally naming men responsible), her town of origin, current address and physical description. Julia Grant of Dean Street, Soho, had dazzling white teeth and blue eyes.

A few are illustrated, e.g. Rachel Rutherford, alias Mrs Sinclair. Is she the lady aged 25 living on 'independent means' in St George's Terrace? Many predictably plied their trade under a pseudonym.

However, it's easy to defame perfectly respectable women earning an honest living. Madame Wohlegmuth, for instance, was enumerated, 1841, as a dressmaker in Somerset Street, the very heart of this infamous area. Tracing her records, Madeleine née Chevallier from Paris married widower Gustav Wohlgemuth by licence in 1824. By 1851, she and daughters Maria and Agatha had moved to 57 New Bond Street (HO107/1475/429/12) running a successful couturier business employing three women and still there in 1861. Photos and other ephemera from descendants are on Ancestry's public member trees.

Prostitutes congregated where there was trade, many travelling a considerable distance from their original homes. Economic migrants and Irish women escaping famine across the water arrived in Liverpool and London; Scottish women moved south. One giveaway is a female ancestor living in a port or vicinity of a dockyard; another, several young women born around the country sharing a house, or a hoard of illegitimate children. Alarms should ring if your ancestor lives in her own establishment describing herself as 'of independent means' or 'FS' (female servant, 1841 census only) surrounded by others in the same situation.

In certain London streets, especially Regent Street, police policy was to arrest unaccompanied women. Seamstress Elizabeth Cass was accused of soliciting 28 June 1887 and became a *cause célèbre* when she sued her arresting officer, PC Endacott, for perjury. The jury is still out as to whether she was a prostitute or not.

King's Cross in the 1870s and 1880s was another disreputable haunt for brothels and prostitutes. Newspapers constantly berated police for providing insufficient officers when women harassed local respectable men. *The Times*, 15 March 1889, reports Marlborough Street Police Court trial of Lilly Montague, 26, from Trevor Square and her friend Mabel Graham, also 26, living in Lodge Road, St Johns, arrested for 'assaulting Captain Reginald Kays of the 5th

Fusiliers'. Lilly was fined 40s or a month imprisonment if she didn't pay up. For her 'unprovoked attack' Mabel was fined 20s or fourteen days' imprisonment.

Because they worked outside society and the law, many had short, tragic lives. Ann Kelly, born c1834 in Ireland, lodged in the King's Head public house, Brook, Chatham, in 1861. Brook was a notoriously rough area, and, although listed in the census without an occupation, Ann was a prostitute (as were possibly the other four girls lodging there, all aged under 29). The *Chatham News*, 26 April 1862, reports her month's imprisonment with hard labour at Maidstone jail for 'drunk and riotous' behaviour. Two years later, 19 February 1864, she lived behind The Bell public house and was 'seized and assaulted in a most outrageous manner' by two soldiers lying in wait for her; Peter Mooney, 20, and Joseph Mulqueen, 24. Because of her 'loose character' and 'uncorroborated' account (she was alone in the room with them) the men were acquitted of rape but jailed for eighteen months with hard labour for assault. By March 1865, she had died from exposure.

LOCK HOSPITALS

On the night of the 1861 census, six young women were patients in Manchester's lock hospital conveniently located next to Deansgate police station. In charge was blacksmith's wife, 46-year-old matron, Margaret Naylor (HO9/2943/20/34). These hospitals treated sexual diseases, mainly syphilis. The title 'lock hospital' was not because patients were locked up, but because their original purpose was treating leprosy with locks (rags) of material covering lesions.

The eldest patient, Matilda Kirby, 27, from New Mills (about 19 miles from Manchester), worked in a cotton mill; the youngest at 16, a general servant from Northwich (23 miles away). Throstle spinner (cotton mill worker), Martha Arnfield, 22, originated all the way from Hull and all but one were unmarried. I don't like casting aspersions but a single woman in a lock hospital was a prostitute either full or part-time.

Fast forward ten years to the same Manchester lock hospital;

Margaret Naylor, alongside now-retired blacksmith husband, is still matron. The patients have soared to twenty-five, their occupations semi or low skilled in textile mills or servants, ages ranging from 35 to 14 with the majority in their early twenties. They came from Scotland (the youngest, domestic servant Mary Anderson), Ireland, Liverpool, Blackpool and Lincolnshire as well as closer to home. All were unmarried. Why so many more women there?

CONTAGIOUS DISEASES ACTS

The answer lay with the punitive Contagious Diseases Acts (1864, 1866, 1869, repealed 1886). By 1864, the proliferation of prostitution was deemed so unmanageable that, in an attempt to eradicate or at least control the rampant rise of venereal disease (VD) in the army and navy, any woman suspected of soliciting in naval towns Chatham, Devonport, Portsmouth or army town Aldershot was arrested and forcibly examined by a male doctor for signs of VD. A positive result meant incarceration and treatment in a lock hospital for up to three months plus compulsory registration as prostitute.

Over the next five years, more towns, two in Ireland, were added with a five-mile catchment area encircling each town. Detention was increased to up to nine months. By 1882, the Act covered the original four towns plus Canterbury, Gravesend and Sheerness, Colchester, Dover, Maidstone, Plymouth, Shorncliffe (Folkestone), Southampton, Winchester, Windsor and Woolwich – with constant exhortations to get it extended everywhere. It was also implemented in India and Caribbean islands governed by the British Empire.

Ruthlessly policed by plain clothes undercover agents roaming specific areas, unaccompanied women were harassed and detained. If accused of being a 'common prostitute', she was subjected to fortnightly examinations intimate enough to induce miscarriage and compared to rape. Some innocent women were maliciously accused of prostitution, inadvertently losing both reputation and *virgo intacta*.

In 1869, the Ladies National Association for the Repeal of the Contagious Diseases Act (LNA) was co-founded by Manchester-born Elizabeth Clarke Wolstenholme Elmy (1833–1918, secretary on the Married Women's Property Committee, 1867 to 1882) and clergyman's wife, Josephine Butler (née Gray, 1828–1906). Both risked reputation and social ostracism by defending prostitutes and demanding the repeal of the Act. Butler specifically objected to the hypocrisy and double standards by which women were punished for actions perpetrated by men. She quoted a Canterbury prostitute jailed rather than submit to an internal examination because, only days earlier, the woman had been paid a few pennies by the very trial's male magistrate for her professional services. The going price for a Manchester street prostitute, Butler revealed, might only be 2d. With police harassment, constant threat of violence from punters, the risk of disease and pregnancy plus illegal abortions, a prostitute's life was wretched and dangerous beyond description.

In 1882, a select committee formed entirely of men was set up to investigate whether or not the Contagious Diseases Act should be reformed or abolished.

Eliza Southby, 22, a resident of Dover, a port under the jurisdiction of the Act, found herself an unwilling celebrity. An innocent victim of the Act, she'd been tailed by plain clothes policemen, hunted, harassed and finally accused of prostitution. Supported by expert witness, Josephine Butler, she gave her testimony to the committee. Repeated word for word, the whole sorry caboodle and extent of Eliza's ordeal is revealed in *The Report from the Select Committee on Contagious Diseases Act, 1882*, found online at *https://archive.org/details/reportfromselect1882grea*.

Eliza Southby (also documented as Elizabeth Jane Southey) was described by police reports as 5ft 6 or 7 inches tall, fair complexioned, fair haired with a fringe. Her father William, a publican at the Duke of York, Snargate Street, had died in November 1879 leaving, according to probate, under £200 to his widow Jane. Eliza lodged with Mrs Ford at 3 Adrian Street, two doors from Eliza's grandfather. To help ends meet, the widow took in mangling, and Eliza helped her.

Several officers from the Metropolitan Police gave statements including a Constable Matthews. He explained she had been under their surveillance for several months 'entertaining' soldiers and sailors in quiet, lonely places. Visiting her lodgings, he accused her of leading an 'immoral life', commanded her to attend a meeting at 5 Seven Stars Street, Dover, at 12 noon on 19 April 1882 in order, it transpired, to examine her under the Contagious Diseases Act. During his statement, Matthews admitted his 'notion of a common prostitute is by seeing her continually with different men and going into different out of the way places'.

The truth, however, was significantly different. Eliza was a general servant working in town for several respectable families to support her bed-ridden aunt and 82-year-old grandfather. Paying him 2s a week for food, 'as much as I could afford', she ate her meals there and did his housework.

Contradicting the 'different men' theory, she was engaged to her boyfriend of four months, Stephen Bates, an artillery man (gunner of the 12th battery, 11th Brigade, based at Dover). This was whom the over-zealous policeman had followed. Eliza insisted there was never any 'impropriety' and the 'other men' were his friends she had met whilst accompanying her fiancé. Apart from one visit to the music hall with Bates, she invariably went to bed before ten and the 'different out of the way places' were where she worked.

The case was summarily dismissed but at what expense to Eliza's reputation and future? Her name was exposed in local syndicated newspapers, *Canterbury Journal, Kentish Times and Farmers' Gazette* (6 May 1882) plus others further afield. The collateral damage affected not just her, whose reputation was shattered, but also Stephen Bates. I found neither record of their marriage nor a feasible Stephen Bates marrying anyone else.

When Eliza Southey was accused of prostitution, there were but thirty-two women on the police register for Dover. In the twenty years from the start of the Contagious Diseases Act in 1864 to 1882, only seventy women in total had been committed for the entire areas of Folkestone, Canterbury and thirty-nine for Dover. Butler and Elmy's campaign plus the unjustified accusation against Eliza Southey resulted in the 1886 repeal of these Acts.

Helen Mather's website dedicated to Josephine Butler is at *https://josephinebutlerpage.com*. Butler's letters plus LNA archives are at the Woman's Library at the LSE *www.lse.ac.uk/library/Home.aspx*. The Women's Library catalogue is at *https://twl-calm.library. lse.ac.uk/CalmView* but, as most material is in close access, a visit is required to consult them. Also held at the LSE is the Charles Booth Archive containing references to prostitution in Victorian London, see *https://booth.lse.ac.uk*.

VAGRANTS, HAWKERS AND COSTERMONGERS

The Vagrancy Act 1824 made it illegal to sleep rough or beg. Synonyms for beggar include vagabond, cadger (in Victorian slang a homeless person making money any way they could), peddler, market man or huskster/huckster.

It required a licence to casually sell goods in the street, either as hawker or costermonger, and it was an offence not to have one. There were also periods when hawking was illegal – Manchester banned them from 1838. Many found themselves prosecuted for vagrancy or not having a hawkers' licence.

Surviving licences are held locally and information includes distinguishing marks to identify the hawker as the person to whom the licence was issued. Local newspapers, as always, are another source, and magistrate and prison records highlight an ancestor who went to court and possibly prison for illegal trading. For an ancestor accused of illegal hawking, there is no licence . . .

INFANTICIDE AND BABY FARMING

If a woman needed to keep her servant's job, or hold tight to her reputation as a single woman, killing an unwanted new-born baby, especially an illegitimate one, was an act of personal survival. A sad indictment is the number of young unmarried women executed for killing an illegitimate child, with twenty hanged between 1800 and 1868. Their back stories are poignant and/or distressing.

In one notorious case, 'the body in the parcel', Ada Annie Williams, 26, was convicted at London's Central Criminal Court

(Old Bailey) in December 1913 for murdering her illegitimate 4-year-old son, John Patrick Harvey Dunn, born before she married. Blaming him for ruining her subsequent marriage, she strangled the child and attempted to burn his body. On conviction, she claimed she was pregnant at which point a jury of matrons was called and declared this true. A son was born in Holloway Prison a few months later and Ada discharged on licence in 1921.

For leniency, a woman could plead puerperal insanity although, should she be convicted of infanticide using this defence as mitigating circumstances, she kept her life often at the expense of incarceration in an asylum. The *Warwick and Warwickshire Advertiser*, 11 May 1867, reports the inquest of one-month-old George, son of Eliza and George Barnwell, drowned in a canal lock under suspicious circumstances. Eliza was exonerated by the jury for being 'low spirited' and 'did not appear to have any ill feeling toward it'. The verdict was accidental death.

In convictions for mass infanticide, perpetrators were invariably women and many were 'baby farmers'. This pejorative term, coined in *The Times* in the late 1860s, came to mean people who took in children for payment. Food, clothing, heat and medicine cost money. Child mortality was rife. Who was to dispute a child dying under their care especially if it was conveniently illegitimate?

It was not illegal to send out a baby to be nursed or looked after during the day whilst mother worked. In middle and upper-class families, it was common to send infants away until they were weaned (Chapter 1). The problem arose when a woman couldn't afford to keep a baby and paid someone to look after or 'adopt' it for a fixed fee. If an insurance policy towards burial was bought, potential income could be doubled. Burial clubs, even for small babies, paid up to £5 for funeral expenses for a subscription of a mere farthing or halfpenny a week.

Symptoms of arsenic poisoning (found in products for vermin control) were similar to dysentery and gastritis and difficult to diagnose. By the 1840s, parliament was debating the high incidence of child deaths. There were attempts at legislation and in 1855

(Friendly Societies Act), insurance payments were restricted to £4 for children under 12.

Examples of notorious baby farmers are:

- Charlotte Winsor from Torquay, Devon, 'a hag who lived by strangling babies' (*Dublin Evening Mail*, August 1865). Charged Mary Jane Harris 3s a week to care for Mary's son Thomas Edwin Gibson Harris but, when Mary could no longer afford to pay, suffocated Thomas, wrapped him in newspaper and dumped him on the side of the road. For £3 to £5, Winsor disposed of 'children whom their mothers found it inconvenient to support'. Execution commuted to penal servitude for life, May 1866.
- 'Brixton Baby Farmer' Margaret Waters, 35, executed 11 November 1870, Surrey County Prison, for poisoning several infants with laudanum and poor-quality food, insisting they died of thrush or diarrhoea. Pleading guilty to receiving money under false pretences, she is quoted saying (*Norfolk News*, 15 October 1870) 'The parents were really the sinners' for 'getting rid of their illegitimate children'.
- Annie Tooke, 40, executed Exeter, Devon, 11 August 1879, for smothering, dismembering and throwing the remains of six-month illegitimate and 'malformed' Reginald Hede into a mill stream. Having been paid £12 a year to look after him, she blamed the child's natural mother, Mary Hoskings. After the inquest, the jurymen gave their fees to Annie's four orphaned children.
- 'Reading Baby Farmer' Amelia Dyer née Amelia Elizabeth Hobley, aged about 59, executed Newgate, June 1896. Accused of killing between 200 and 400 largely illegitimate children by neglect and starvation. Under a variety of aliases, she was paid around £10 to adopt each one. None survived very long.

These and other cases are reported in contemporary newspapers.

PUNISHMENT
Capital punishment
By 1815, under what became known as 'The Bloody Code', capital punishment was the sentence for over 288 crimes including theft of property worth more than 5s, uttering (the passing of forged documents with intent to defraud) or cutting down a young tree. In 1823, the number of proscribed crimes punishable by death was reduced. From this date, theft of property had to exceed a value of more than £10 to risk that penalty.

Execution was no respecter of gender but considerably more men received the ultimate deterrent. In 1815, fifty-four were hanged but only four women – for murder, attempted murder (a capital crime until 1861), arson and petty/petit treason. Petty treason was an offence in which a subordinate (wife or servant) betrayed their superior (husband or employer); effectively, if a wife murdered her husband or a servant murdered her employer. The penalty was particularly harsh, with an offender publicly dragged to the gallows to be hanged and often dissected afterwards. The Offences Against the Person Act 1828 simplified the law by repealing petty treason and replacing it with murder. However, a man killing his wife for her adultery could plead manslaughter (provocation and loss of control) until as recently as the Coroners and Justice Act 2009.

The last female public execution was that of Frances Kidder, 25, outside Maidstone Prison, 2 April 1868, for drowning her stepdaughter aged 11 in a ditch.

Richard Clark's dedicated capital punishment website *www. capitalpunishmentuk.org* has a plethora of detail with date, name, age, place of execution and crime. The more infamous crimes (often gruesome) have their own pages. Contemporary newspapers enjoyed sensationalised detail and *www.oldbaileyonline.org* has transcripts of trials at London's Central Criminal Court.

A woman who declared herself pregnant at a trial had her execution delayed until after the birth. Dating from 1387, 'pleading the belly' was corroborated by examination by a 'jury of matrons' to confirm her condition. If she became pregnant again, the sentence was recommuted. Many Victorian courts preferred clemency, i.e. transportation or imprisonment.

Transportation

Seven out of eight transportees were male. The original destination was America until the War of Independence when British convicts were no longer welcome. The first voyage down-under, the First Fleet, transported 548 men, 188 women and 25 children on eleven ships from Portsmouth to Australia, in May 1787. Only six ships conveyed convicts. The maximum sentence to Australia was life (minimum, two years) and, just as execution had been, was regarded as a disincentive to commit murder and other serious crimes. However, many convicts were transported for what we now regard as petty offences – theft over a value of 5s for instance. By the 1840s, as it was realised that transportation wasn't a deterrent, it fell out of favour but, although theoretically abolished by the Penal Servitude Act of 1857, a few transportations continued until 1868.

Women prisoners were the minority in Australia. Between 1788 and 1842, although 80,000 convicts were transported to New South Wales only 15 per cent were women. An Australian website tracing transportees is *https://convictrecords.com.au*. Convicted at Stamford Quarter Sessions, Lincoln, with seven years' penal servitude, Harriet Smith, alias Jane Smith, arrived in New South Wales after a five-month voyage on *Henry Wellesley*, 22 December 1837. Accompanying her were 139 women convicted for various offences including Sarah Allen, Ann Andrews and Mary Ann Bigwell convicted at the Central Criminal Court, London, plus others from e.g. Worcester, Buckinghamshire, Shropshire, York, Glamorgan, Norfolk and Devon.

It's possible to discover their offence, especially if they were tried at London's Central Criminal Court where records are online *www.oldbaileyonline.org*. The aforementioned Mary Ann Bigwell, an under-housemaid, was convicted 12 June 1837 for stealing '2 sovereigns, 2 shillings and a £10 and £5 banknote' ten days earlier from her master, Henry Hall Esq of Langham Place, St Marylebone.

Aged 24 at the time of the offence, she was transported for life, 'recommended to mercy . . . in consequence of the temptation and her previous good character'. Added genealogical information is supplied by mention of her aunt, Amelia Newland, who provided a good character reference at the trial. Mary Ann was transported 17 July 1837, disembarking just before Christmas.

Another free website *www.prov.vic.gov.au* lists convict's name, date of sailing and ship. Emma R Miller sailed on convict ship *The Persian* in December 1852 and there's a page reference to the register. A link to *www.blaxland.com/ozships/events/8/708.htm#68309* (main website *www.blaxland.com*) shows *The Persian* had 619 passengers, sailed from London 22 September and arrived in Melbourne 27 December 1852 where it was put into quarantine for three days.

The TNA *www.nationalarchives.gov.uk/help-with-your-research/ research-guides/free-online-records-digital-microfilm* has free to download microfilm records as part of their digital microfilm project and HO10 has lists of male, female convicts and former convicts in New South Wales and Tasmania for 1789–1854 at *http://discovery.nationalarchives. gov.uk/browse/r/h/C8874*. You might find information on sentence, employment, settlement in the country, whether they later acquired land or cattle, pardons granted, general musters and census records for 1828. Download instructions are given on the website. A reminder – most convicts were men.

Ancestry holds, *inter alia*, Australian Convict Transportation Registers which includes Fleets and Ships, 1791–1868 *https://search. ancestry.co.uk/search/db.aspx?dbid=1180* and reveals name of convict, date and place of conviction, term of sentence, name of ship on which they sailed, departure date and colony they were sent to. The New South Wales, Australia Convict Ship Muster Rolls and Related Records, 1790–1849 *https://search.ancestry.co.uk/search/ db.aspx?dbid= 1211* consists of ship muster lists of convicts transported from England to New South Wales as well as Canada, India, South Africa, Van Diemen's Land and other parts of Australia. The aforementioned Mary Ann Bigwell is listed but with the same information as the free Australian convict site *https://convictrecords.com.au.*

It goes without saying that transportees, even with the shortest term, didn't expect to return home. For a wife whose husband had been transported, life was precarious without the main breadwinner. The local vicar often took a pragmatic view of potential bigamy (Chapter 1); after all, who knew if her husband had survived the many months at sea?

Imprisonment

For a woman to go to prison, she had to be sentenced at a trial. Petty sessions, held several times a week, were adjudicated by Justices of the Peace. Here, as today, all allegations had a preliminary hearing where lesser cases were summarily and immediately resolved but more serious ones referred upwards to Quarter Sessions held, as the name suggests, every quarter. Assizes dealt with the most heinous.

A plaintiff, the police or member of the public, made allegations about an issue or crime; a woman appealing for maintenance for a bastard child or abandonment; a claim of theft or assault. The magistrate settled payment (10s a week was customary for an illegitimate child in the 1880s), awarded a short prison sentence or fine. Before 1848, few petty sessions records survive. Magistrates' records may be held locally and many have neither been transcribed nor digitised, for example, at the time of writing, Stockport Magistrate Court Records for the petty sessions e.g. 1880–1914 and beyond. These records are held off site and Stockport Library required two days' notice to retrieve them. Information in the leather-bound, hand-written tomes is as follows:

- date of appearance at the petty sessions
- official case number
- name of informant or complainant (e.g. 'police' – in many cases, it was the policeman's name; someone bringing charges of assault; name of woman appealing for bastardy payments)
- name of defendant, age if under 16

- nature of offence or matter of complaint
- minute of adjudication (including comments like *non-appearance*; if a warrant has been executed, fine and amount, imprisonment and length, dismissal, withdrawal, bail, remand)
- adjudicating justices (names of the men hearing the cases).

Newspapers often reported magistrates' court hearings. The first female magistrate was Councillor Ada Summers née Broome (1861–1944), appointed magistrate/JP for Stalybridge, Cheshire, in 1919.

The assizes dealt with more serious cases. The TNA's help-sheet is at *www.nationalarchives.gov.uk/help-with-your-research/research-guides/criminal-trials-assize-courts-1559-1971*. Remember, criminals are dishonest, tell lies and use aliases!

Prison life was appalling. Quaker Elizabeth Fry née Gurney (1780–1845) first visited Newgate prison in 1813, finding terrifying conditions where over 300 women and children, some convicted, others awaiting trial, were confined willy nilly in two wards and two cells. Another prison, Millbank Penitentiary, Pimlico, London, was built in 1816, completed 1821, and for a time, England's largest prison housing over 1,000 prisoners including women, many transferred from all around the country. Achieving notoriety for atrocious conditions, it closed in 1890. Tate Britain occupies the site.

A female ancestor incarcerated on census night will be recorded as 'prisoner' although, like residents in a workhouse, she may be listed as initials as at Millbank, 1861, where only staff were named in full. Woking Female Prison, 1871, however, names 'convicts' hailing from all regions across the UK with former trade, age and marital status. Seamstresses, laundrywomen, charwomen are common. Middle-class women were unlikely to find themselves in such a pickle.

Licences of Parole for Female Convicts 1853–71, 1883–7, held at TNA are on Ancestry. Search by name to find personal details, reports on behaviour whilst in prison and photographs from 1871. I've seen online parole licences consisting of twenty-one pages and considerable information. As befits criminals, many women used several aliases to avoid detection and, as today, received increased sentences if habitual offenders.

Mary Higham (alias Cooper) was sentenced to seven years' penal servitude at Manchester on 26 June 1865 for 'Larceny from the person: stealing a purse from John Jackson containing £3100' (a huge sum). She was released, 21 July 1869, aged 27, on licence (No. 3404) from Woking Female Prison (a long way from home) to husband John living at 18 Butterworth Court, Byron Street, Manchester. Failure to adhere to her licence conditions meant an immediate return to gaol.

Her official record informs us she was married with two children and no trade. She'd never had scarlet fever, smallpox, or epilepsy and had been vaccinated (smallpox, Chapter 1). She could read and write, was Roman Catholic, and had three previous convictions. May 1860, she was acquitted of stealing a watch but convicted for the same offence the following month and received six months. As married housekeeper Mary Jane Cooper with one child, she was committed February 1861 for three years for stealing a purse containing £175 in bank notes and gold from Peter Hopwood Moore and despatched to Millbank Prison. To aid future identification and detection, she is described as: dark complexion, black hair, dark brown eyes, pockmarks on forehead (so much for vaccination), facial scars from cuts and boils, two moles on left arm and pierced ears. She stood 5 ft 2½ in tall. For her final conviction, she spent one month and twenty-one days in Manchester City Gaol before transferring to Millbank Prison (received 8 August 1865), Parkhurst in October and Woking Female Prison April 1869. Other details relate to her behaviour in prison.

A later example of a parole licence, and one containing a photo, is Mary Ann Edwards/Mary Ann Connor (also known as Mary Ann Smith and Mary Ann Leeke; good luck untangling this if you are her descendant), born c1850, convicted of larceny and receiving stolen goods, 9 August 1880.

Anyone held in a police prison overnight is named on the census. At Deansgate Police Station, 1861, Scottish bonnet trimmer

Greater Manchester Police Museum, Newton Street © Adèle Emm

Catherine Anderson, 20, is held alongside hawker's wives Julia Gorman, 35, from Ireland and Sarah Walker, 39, from Salford. A handwritten note to the left of the enumerator's record states 'prisoners locked up on Sunday night, 7th'.

There was often charitable support for young girls released from prison and you might find an ancestor there. One such, the Elizabeth Fry Refuge at 195 Mare Street, Hackney, founded 1845 after Fry's death, supported girls over the age of 11. Under the auspices of Norfolk-born (like Fry herself) widowed matron Susanna High, twenty 'inmates' ranging in age from 11 to 25 from Ireland, Bristol, Wiltshire and local Hackney lived there in 1851 (HO107/1506/ 157/29). These highly regarded places were well sought-after, offering a second chance with training for poverty-stricken but generally honest girls convicted for stealing food, wearing another person's clothes or pawning someone else's possessions – trivial transgressions of young desperate women. By 1881, Elizabeth Fry's Refuge was neighboured by all-female Tre-Wint Industrial School three doors down the road. The helm at Fry's Refuge was taken by matron Esther Strange, two assistants (teaching needlework and laundry) plus twenty-three female residents aged 16 to 32, now not 'inmates' but the more respectable cook and parlour maid etc. (RG11/311/15/21). For further information about the home, see Claudia Jessop's contribution to Hackney Society's webpage at *www.hackneysociety.org/page_id_259.aspx*. The Refuge's records, including casebooks from 1849 containing some individual girls' details, are held at Hackney; see TNA for details.

Greater Manchester Police Museum and Archives *www.gmp museum.co.uk* holds 'mug shots' of some former prisoners largely from the 1870s. Its Flickr page with a historical album and photos is a private file and you must visit the museum to view them.

The Thieves Book containing offences committed from the 1870s, only viewable at the Police Museum, contains eighty-three photos, admittedly male skewed, but there are some women. It's a headache to decipher a real name when so many used a multitude of aliases to obfuscate a felonious background. Take Mary Connelly whose trade was 'thief'. Her aliases were so numerous they filled two columns: Mullins, Baxter, Hilda Ellis, Matthews, Mary Ellen O'Laughlin, Eliza Buxton, Ellen Summers are just a few! Born in Ireland, she was 46 in 1893 (another lie?) with grey eyes and fresh complexion. The 'marks' column, by which police could identify her as one and the same person, lists scars here, there and everywhere. A scrapper. Her offences followed her round the country from Birmingham, Northwich, Manchester, Liverpool, Sandbach, Chester, Leeds and Salford, with prison sentences ranging from fourteen days to twelve months (October 1893).

The Manchester Police Museum also holds two 'Criminal Albums'. Book 1 contains details and photographs of 271 criminals with book 2 holding sixty-eight photographs albeit mainly men. The Manchester City Police Identification Album from the 1870s holds 207 photos. Its archives and website also have a history of the Women's Police force.

Women's first official contribution to the force was as volunteers in 1914 following the exodus of men to the front in the First World War, but their involvement was acknowledged from at least the 1890s when women, often police officers' wives, attended to the welfare and supervision of women prisoners in police station cells, often described as matron. Records countrywide show policemen's wives taking on the role of searching female prisoners and delivering food to them.

The Metropolitan Habitual Criminal and Drunkards Registers for 100,000 criminals (1881–1925, ref; MEPO 6) are held at TNA subject to a seventy-five-year closure. Anyone imprisoned for more than two offences following the 1871 Prevention of Crime Act was included on this register. Information is similar to that recorded in Manchester Police Museum Criminals Album.

The Sussex Police Museum, based in Brighton Town Hall, also holds useful insights into female criminals at *www.oldpolicecells museum.org.uk*.

Prison records are held locally and some have been transcribed, found, for instance, in the Manchester Collection on FindMyPast (court and prison). The transcription, as always, has less information than the original often just one click away.

The records for Belle Vue Prison, Manchester (a short-term prison for men and women), are part of the Manchester Prison Registers

1847–81 available at Manchester Central Library (free) and FindMyPast. They reveal:

- name
- age last birthday
- conviction, i.e. larceny
- place of birth
- last or usual residence
- professed trade or occupation
- marks upon the person and remarks (e.g. height, colour of hair, eyes, vaccination marks and scars)
- extent of instruction; as in 'read', 'imperfect' or 'none', giving a level of their literacy
- married/single and number of children
- religion
- parents still alive
- sentence, e.g. nine months hard labour
- date of incarceration
- number of prior convictions (the most I saw for a woman was fifty-six)
- letters sent or received plus dates
- date of discharge – i.e. discharged, sent to another prison, died in custody

Marital Coercion

Two mugshots in the Manchester City Police Identification Album are of Ann Henry alias Annie Keenan (prison number 93676) and Jane Grey alias Gaylor alias 'Hoppy's woman' (93677). According to handwritten notes, both were associated with the 'Montague, Coyne and Gaylor gang', convicted March 1874. Ann Henry received fifteen months' hard labour and Jane Grey/Gaylor, nine. Their actual offence isn't revealed but, delving into contemporary newspapers, I discovered they attempted to use 'marital coercion' as a defence against 'breaking and entering' and 'larceny'.

Under common law, this was a defence whereby, should a

married woman commit a crime in the presence of her husband, it was presumed 'she acted under his coercion and excludes her from punishment'. If she could prove he was (a) present when she committed the crime and (b) he had pressurised her into it, she could be acquitted. The defence was invalid for murder or treason.

According to contemporary newspapers, the gang, three men and our two women, were indicted for the Great Jewellery Robbery in Manchester, March 1874, when jewellery, watches and rings worth over £2,000 were stolen from Lewis S Knight's shop, Shudehill. Published details described the overnight casing of the shop, the two women standing guard and one robber clubbed by a policeman to the ground for producing a revolver.

The women's defence hinged on marital coercion and, insisting they were gang members' wives, both factory operative Ann, 23, and milliner Jane, 24, pleaded not guilty. Ann professed to be married to saddler Alfred Coyne, 21, in Birmingham in 1867. Jane produced a

	REGISTRATION DISTRICT					CHORLTON
1874	DEATH in the Sub-district of Ardwick				in the	Coun

Columns:–	1	2	3	4	5	6
No.	When and where died	Name and surname	Sex	Age	Occupation	Cause of death
	15th September 1874 403 City Gaol Hyde Road	Jane Grey	Female	24 years	Single woman Milliner a Prisoner in the said Gaol	Natural Disease to wit Consumption

Detail Jane Grey's death certificate, 15 September 1874. Manchester city gaol, consumption. GRO

certificate proving marriage to an Elijah Gaylor at St Sepulchres, London, 20 July 1868. Prosecution was not convinced. Both Alfred Coyne and Ann Henry were under age at marriage. Also, notwithstanding Gaylor's suspicious name change on the marriage certificate or being eighteen years Jane's senior, their final clincher was that identity could not be proven by a certificate. For fun, I checked marriages on the Civil Registration Marriage Index – not there. However, an Elijah Gaylor married Mary Ann Wolfe, September 1868 – and he names Mary Ann as wife on his admittance to Belle Vue Prison. Although the three men were sentenced to ten, twelve and fourteen years' imprisonment, the women received lesser sentences so the plea had been effective. With four prior convictions in Scotland counting against her, Ann received fifteen months, Jane nine. Aged 26, she died of consumption before completing her sentence.

Some family history societies, e.g. Wiltshire, publish 'black sheep' records. Oxford Black Sheep Publications' *Oxford Gaol Prisoner Portraits, 1870–1881* (vol. 8, Oxford Crimes, 2011) has photographs. Family history societies are a fount of knowledge for transcribed records and publications are listed online. As always, try TNA; their help-sheet is at *www.nationalarchives.gov.uk/help-with-your-research/research-guides/prisoners-or-prison-staff.* Online subscription services provide constantly updated criminal records, e.g. Ancestry has Home Office records for 1791–1892 and FindMyPast has after-trial calendars of prisoners 1855–1931 (CRIM 9): Home Office calendars of prisoners 1868–1929 (HO 140); registers of criminal petitions 1797–1853 (HO 19) and lists of prisoners tried at Newgate 1782–1853 (HO 77). As TNA reminds you, not everything is online and they recommend the local CRO.

Newspapers are invaluable and often provide further details for researchers to head towards surviving court records (often not indexed).

To reiterate, hardened criminals are difficult to trace because they dissembled about everything including name, place and date of birth which they may not actually have known.

PLACES TO VISIT

Bodmin Jail *www.bodminjail.org*
Old Police Cells Museum, Brighton, Sussex
www.oldpolicecellsmuseum.org.uk
Greater Manchester Police Museum and Archives
www.gmpmuseum.co.uk, open Tuesdays free admission; private
tours and access to archives by appointment only
Lancaster Castle and prison *www.lancastercastle.com/tours-visits*
Ripon Prison and Police Museum
http://riponmuseums.co.uk/museums/prison_police_museum

Bibliography and Further Reading

Acton, William, *Prostitution Considered in its Moral, Social, and Sanitary Aspects, in London and Other Large Cities and Garrison Towns*, 1870; found online at *archive.org*

Ager, Adrian, and Lee, Catherine, *Prostitution in the Medway Towns*, 1860–85 at *www.localpopulationstudies.org.uk/ PDF/ LPS83/Prostitution-in%20the-Medway-towns.pdf*

Chambers, Jill, *www.black-sheep-search.co.uk*

Chesney, Kellow, *The Victorian Underworld*, Pelican, 1989

Clark, Richard, *Women and the Noose*, History Press, 2008

Duckworth, Jeannie, *Fagin's Children: Criminal Children in Victorian England*, Continuum, 2002

Flanders, Judith, 'Prostitution', British Library article on prostitution in Victorian literature *www.bl.uk/romantics-and-victorians/articles/prostitution*

Funnyman, Roger, Hon FLG (i.e. anonymous), *A Swell's Night Guide through the Metropolis*, London, 1841

Grenville, Kate, *The Secret River*, Canongate, 2005, novel about transportation to Australia

Horn, Pamela, *Young Offenders*, Amberley, 2010

Johnston, Helen, *Crime in England 1815–1880: Experiencing the Criminal Justice System*, Routledge, 2015

Jones, Steve, booklets on local criminal history such as *Birmingham . . . The Sinister Side*; other areas include Nottingham,

Manchester, London, Lancashire, Yorkshire, Northumberland and Durham, Wicked Publications

Logan, William, *An Exposure of Female Prostitution in London, Leeds and Rochdale, and Especially in the City of Glasgow*, Glasgow, 1843

Mathers, Helen, *Patron Saint of Prostitutes: Josephine Butler and a Victorian Scandal*, History Press, 2014. Her website on Butler see *https://josephinebutlerpage.com/about*

Mayhew, Henry, *London Labour and the London Poor*, Charles Griffin & Co., 1864/5 (orig. publ. as newspaper/periodical articles, 1851)

Priestley, Philip, *Victorian Prison Lives, English Prison Biography, 1830–1914*, Pimlico, 1999

Report from the Select Committee on Contagious Diseases Act, 1882 online at *https://archive.org/details/reportfromselect1882grea*

Sharp, Ingrid, and Jordan, Jane, eds, *Josephine Butler and the Prostitution Campaigns*, Routledge, 2003

Thomas, Donald, *The Victorian Underworld*, John Murray, 2003

Wade, Stephen, *Tracing Your Criminal Ancestors*, Pen & Sword, 2009

Chapter 4

DAILY LIFE

A woman's daily life was determined by her class. At best, a working-class woman's life was drudgery: washing, house-work, raising children and perhaps putting in a full day's work if augmenting her husband's income in a cottage industry or at the factory. Poor families had scarce possessions and few rooms in which to keep them. During periods of economic hardship, two (or more) families might live and sleep in one room which, in cities like Manchester, could be a purpose-built underground cellar incorporated into a house by an unscrupulous landlord. Simplistically speaking, the more rooms a family inhabited, the wealthier they were.

HOUSING
The supremely wealthy owned their homes, large piles constructed or adapted to their taste. For the aristocracy, we only need visit Britain's stately homes to appreciate their standard of living. Few others owned their house. A builder might erect a row of terraces and occupy the end house, often slightly larger than the rest, collecting rent from his tenants at the end of each week. Even the middle class rented but had a wider choice of houses and locations to choose from.

For anyone who did own their home, paperwork went with purchase and, if it survives, is worth examining. Land registration today is electronic but I was lucky enough to be offered the conveyancing paperwork (which otherwise would have been destroyed) for my 1904 house. Contents include original maps, land and house dimensions, indentures and names of owners. The first was Mrs Elizabeth Johnston, wholesale florist, wife of Francis William Johnston. The cost? £405. This was after 1882 so Mrs Johnson could own property in her own right. She rented it out.

A mill manager and his family might have a large house next to, or even on, the premises of, the mill. The overseer (always male) might lease a house with front and back garden where they grew vegetables.

Once you've found an address for your female ancestor living in London, you might want to check out William Spencer Clark's *The Suburban Homes of London*, 1881, at *https://archive.org/details/ suburbanhomeslo00clargoog*. This fascinating book narrates local history, names prominent residents and addresses and describes streets, many in existence today. Compiled in alphabetical order, it starts with Acton meandering through to Woodford, detailing salubrious and aspirational suburbs plus typical rents. As today, location was key. A home in the Nightingale Lane/Balham Hill Road triangle, Balham, could be rented for £40 to £70 per annum. The more discerning might choose a finer, larger house with an extensive garden towards Upper Tooting and pay well above £100 a year. Benefits and disadvantages to each district are given; the commute from Balham to the City (where the husband worked?) 'though pretty is tedious'. If you had no objection to living near Stockwell's smallpox hospital, a house was under £40 a year. The income for a middle-class family in the late 1870s was £200–£300 per annum so these were well within budget.

The lower classes lived as close as possible to the man's place of work. Some factory owners built houses in the shadow of their mill – even against the wall. No excuse for being late to work especially when the mill-bell tolled the time.

If father changed job, the family moved. The lack of furniture meant an entire household upped sticks quickly and efficiently transporting possessions on a hand cart. Moonlight flits were easy! The 1919 humorous music hall song made famous by Marie Lloyd (1870–1922), 'My old Man said Follow the Van' reflected reality for many.

Families on a low income paid rent weekly, but for those in a slightly higher echelon of life, rent was quarterly or annual. There was a symbiotic relationship between rent, poor law tax and voting rights, but unless a woman was spinster or widow, her name was unlikely to appear on any official paperwork. Her income, however, was an important contribution to family finance and, in many northern mill towns, women constituted the majority of the workforce.

The first useful census for family historians was 1841. Unfortunately, there are three major flaws; ages for adults were rounded down (occasionally up!) to the nearest five years; relationships within households were not shown, and place of birth restricted to whether or not somebody was born within the county or not.

Information collected in subsequent censuses was increasingly sophisticated and by 1911, the number of rooms in a household (including kitchen but excluding scullery, landing, closets and bathroom), plus length of marriage and number of surviving children was recorded.

Back-to-Backs
In many inner cities, back-to-backs, built from the late 1700s, constituted the largest proportion of working-class dwellings. It's estimated three-quarters of Nottingham residents in the 1840s lived in them; two-thirds of Birmingham residents in the 1850s and that there were 18,610 in Liverpool in the 1860s.

One family lived in the front portion and faced the street. Behind their party wall, another household faced either back alley and toilets, or another street. Two or three storeys high, often with a footprint of just eleven square feet, there was a living room, perhaps scullery, on the ground floor and one room on each upper floor.

Many were built around a courtyard, the close or court, and those who lived here entered through a ginnel or gate, sharing the yard with a wash-house (also called the brewhouse), an inevitable washing line, one tap, toilets (little more than open sewers used by

Back-to-backs, Stacksteads, Lancashire. This was the 'back' and overlooked the privies. © Adèle Emm

dozens of people) and dustbins/rubbish tip – the midden. The courtyard was an unofficial children's playground although many preferred the street. No matter the squalor of the building's fabric, women attempted to keep homes spick and span; a curtain at the doorway prevented draughts, hooks on the door supported coats. Working-class houses generally had no carpet but, in late Victorian times, squares of linoleum (invented 1855) or hand-made rag rugs might snuggle in front of the fire or lie beside a bed to protect cold toes using the gazunder, the chamber pot or potty, which 'goes under' the bed.

Rents varied. For back houses in Inge Street, Birmingham, a family might pay 1s 10d a week in 1834 with 2s 6d for one at the front. An end or corner house, deemed more desirable, was perhaps 3s a week. By 1840, rent had increased and a back house might be

2s 6d with a front one 3s 4d. In 1851, widow Sophia Hodson, 33, a pearl button driller, lived with mother Elizabeth James and five children under 16, working in the same industry, at 1 Willmore's Court, Inge Street, built by local man John Willmore.

The only remaining court types in Birmingham are 55–63 and 50–54 Inge Street owned by the National Trust *www.nationaltrust. org.uk/birmingham-back-to-backs.* Tours must be pre-booked.

How would you know if grandma lived in a back-to-back? The address is a clue. In 1901, widow Mary Niblett and two daughters lived at 3 back 163 Fazeley Street, Birmingham. The house behind her party wall fronted Fazeley Street (recorded without 'back'). In 1911, widow Maria Hopkins and four sons shared three rooms in a court-style back-to-back as illustrated in her address; 12 Court 3 House, Inge Street. However, for back-to-backs with a street name to both sides, it must be confirmed against a map – not all 'Back Something Street' was a back-to-back. Back-to-backs still exist. Leeds, Huddersfield and Lancashire, for example, have surviving examples, although some have been knocked through to give more space and light.

Residents of back-to-backs aspired to move to a two-up two-down terrace with its own back yard. Even these came with status. Cheaper houses' front doors opened onto the pavement; rent for a house with pocket-handkerchief front garden was slightly dearer.

Until the 1875 Public Health Act, it wasn't mandatory for houses to have toilets; many didn't have running water either and residents shared seriously unsanitary middens or closets. Following the 1875 Act, councils were compelled to collect refuse and provide street lighting but, crucially, builders must ensure all new houses were well-built, had an internal drainage system and integral water supply. For cheaper houses, this was a cold tap plumbed into a downstairs back room. In working class terraces, the lavatory might be outside, adjoining the back door. Today, their remnants are clearly recognisable from train windows on any suburban line.

It took time before people had these amenities because, of course, older housing stock didn't comply with the new law. Only when a family moved into a new house would they notice the difference. What a transformation on Monday washday (Chapter 5).

It goes without saying that bathing in a two-up two-down shared by two (or more) adults plus several children was a palaver. Through lack of space, for those with the wherewithal to own a tin bath it might be stowed under the stairs or hung on the wall outside the house and brought in on Sunday bath night. Mum heated water on the range, dad got in first followed by everyone else into the increasingly mucky water.

In a large city like Manchester, in the 1911 census, four rooms generally signified a two-up two-down. Take Molyneux Road, Levenshulme, a row of terraces built in the early 1900s. Each house sported a garden bordering the back alley. The majority of residents were families, husbands in skilled labour or manual work, coal merchant, shop assistant, clerk, gas fitter inspector, warehouseman etc., wives at home and two or three children presumably sharing a bedroom. The slightly larger end house was occupied by two sisters, one a telegraphist employed at the Post Office (Chapter 5), and their lodger, a young female teacher.

Contrast them to the Doyle family who, the same year, subsisted at 11 Fawcett Street, Ancoats, an incredibly deprived area of the city where one-up one-down, back-to-backs and cellar dwellings proliferated. Ten people, all Manchester born, were shoe-horned into three rooms. Iron foundry labourer John Doyle and wife Mary, both 50, shared this accommodation with four daughters and four sons, ranging from married 29-year-old daughter (no sign of husband) to 8-year-old son. They survived by hawking flowers, as warehouse packer and as railway carter. Out of their original eleven children, three had died.

In an affluent household, an inside bathroom was standard and the housewife had the added benefit of a female servant, often a young girl, to boil water and clean up afterwards. In a house in my road, 1911, a widow shared seven rooms with her female servant from Kent, 23, who must have relished the space if not the cleaning.

Two-up two-down terraced housing, Levenshulme, Manchester. © Adèle Emm

Lodging and Boarding Houses

Lodging houses were countrywide. Food was included in the rent but there was a huge variation in the standard of such establishments. The more salubrious offered a suite with servants to clean residents' rooms; fictional detective Sherlock Holmes famously shared one with Dr Watson in Baker Street.

'Any ordinary lodging' in a working-class area of London cost £1 18s a week. This was the figure quoted by Charles Dickens' eldest son, Charles Dickens junior (1837–96), compiler of the *Dictionary of Victorian London*, 1882 *http://archive.org/stream/dickenssdictiona 00dick#page/n0/mode/2up*. He considered the 'common lodging house . . . a marvellous revolution in the housing of the London poor'. He was somewhat disingenuous – at worst, such places were appalling, catering for those one rung above vagrancy and homelessness. Although such premises were licensed, most housed all and sundry;

Mary Crockford née Emm ran lodging houses in South and Clarence Parade, Southsea with her husband. This is her enterprise c1907 after his death. Author's collection © Adèle Emm

the down-on-their-luck hugger mugger with thieves, prostitutes, men, women and children higgledy piggedly in one squalid room. One square mile in Whitechapel in the 1880s contained 146 lodging houses accommodating over 6,000 people in total, each paying between 4d and 8d a night (2s 4d to 4s 8d a week). Two of Jack the Ripper's female victims were evicted for not having the funds to pay even this sum.

Almshouses

Often funded by charity and named after the benefactor, these were Victorian old people's homes for the respectable poor, although younger people caring for aged relatives might live there too. Because women were financially less secure than menfolk, older women found themselves, if lucky, residing here.

Potential residents fulfilled specific requirements for an apartment or cottage in these complexes. Many were supported by Guilds like the Company of Victuallers who ran several including Woodland

View, Sheffield (built 1879), or Asylum Road off the Old Kent Road in London (built 1827). To live here, a woman must have worked in the licensing and victualling trade but the widow of a man who'd run a public house or beerhouse might also qualify. Other occupations had similar refuges.

Rents were subsidised, perhaps providing benefits such as free coal, food, a built-in social life, occasionally a warden contributing to a secure, affordable, independent life for residents. However, many came with stringent rules; temperance was common.

Residents of Marlborough Buildings, St Albans, could neither trade from their accommodation nor sublet. If they were away from their residence for more than three days, they must obtain prior permission from the chaplain and if ill or infirm, appoint an approved person to live with them. If they failed to comply, they were 'dismissed'.

The main criterion for admission here was to be over 60 and of limited means. In 1911, retired nurse Miss Lydia Constable (Chapter 5) lived at Number 5. Sharing two rooms two doors down, were sisters, retired schoolteacher Miss Charlotte Stacey, 74, and plain needlewoman Maria Matilda, 60.

A history of Marlborough Buildings is online at *www.stalbans history.org.* For the history of almshouses (the first built from the eleventh century), see the Almshouse Association *www.alms houses.org/history.* The FACHRS 2016 publication, *The British Almshouse, New Perspectives on Philanthropy ca 1400–1914*, edited by Nigel Goose, Helen Caffrey and Anne Langley (ISBN 978-0-9548180-2-9), might be of interest. Wikipedia lists some, but not all, UK almshouses.

Surviving records (e.g. deeds, trustees' archives, minutes of administration, etc.) are in local archives but may not provide much on residents per se. Try TNA as first port of call.

ILLNESS

Before the NHS, doctors were paid for their services, so, because it was a big decision for the working class to call one, they often didn't.

Much of what we shrug off today was potentially fatal especially before the discovery of penicillin (1928) and antibiotics. Burns whilst cooking or cuts could turn septic; tonsillitis, childhood diseases chicken pox, measles and scarlet fever could be disastrous not just for the poor. Old wives' remedies still linger in our psyche: butter on burns (a huge no-no today); feed a cold, starve a fever; vinegar as antiseptic and brown paper on bruises.

Childbirth is a major event in any woman's life. It was costly in more ways than potentially causing her death. Lying-in fees, 1834, were about £1 11s, occasionally covered by Poor Law Guardians if she were destitute. Local women experienced in delivering babies were far cheaper.

In 1890, Liverpool-based Dr Day invoiced tenant farmer, Mr Lamb, £365 6d for treating Lamb's sick wife. Lamb refused to pay more than £180 5s so was sued for the balance. The trial at Liverpool Assizes, reported in *Dorking and Leatherhead Advertiser*, 16 August, quotes Mr Lamb's opinion of the charges. 'Long conversation with Mrs Sykes on behalf of Mrs Lamb with regard to the use of some quack remedy which she recommended and I decline, 10s 6d.' 'Writing a letter to a specialist, 7s 6d.' 'Half a guinea for gossiping.' The fees were compared unfavourably with an attorney's at 6s 8d. After calling independent doctors as witnesses, Dr Day's fees were declared excessive and the court upheld Lamb. We learn neither what ailed the plaintiff's wife nor her outcome.

In 1894, a common fee for a doctor's home visit was 6s 8d (the aforesaid charge for a lawyer) and medicine and drugs, as today, were additional. However, this must be put into context. Rent for a small house in Walthamstow was 10s a week (1881) so if medicine was included, a doctor's visit and treatment was commensurate to one week's rent.

This was untenable for an ordinary household let alone the dirt poor, so families joined a doctor's club paying a few pence a week so, should a doctor's services be required, they were in credit so to speak. In 1888, a middle-class family might budget £33 1s a year for doctor and chemist.

The only option for the desperate was the workhouse infirmary; a decision never taken lightly for this was the last station on the line, although, by the late nineteenth century, conditions had improved and were comparable to a charity hospital. People, however, feared the double stigma of charity and workhouse.

The 1861 Workhouse Register, online at Ancestry, lists every adult pauper (and anyone raised in a workhouse school) who'd been a workhouse inmate for five plus years including reason. Women exceeded men; 7,647 females against 6,569 males. The overwhelming cause of such lengthy incarceration was illness. The register, under county and union, makes sorry reading with reason against each name; *idiot, imbecile, deaf and dumb, weak intellect, old and infirm*, etc. plus time confined in years and months. It's simple to cross-reference names with the census although the policy at some Unions (e.g. Ashton under Lyne and Liverpool) was to enumerate inmates under initials rather than full name, but you can make informed identifications. As always, when people are illiterate, be prepared for differences in spelling even when an individual is clearly the same. Theodosia Rose in Chorlton, Lancashire (*insanity*, resident sixteen years), is enumerated as Theodora Rowse, 30, no trade (RG9/2867/109/29). At the time of writing, this register is not searchable by name.

If medics were out of reach of the poor, dentists also targeted the more affluent. The front page of *Freeman's Journal* advertises the services of male dentist Mr McDonnell, practising in 1906 at 36 Henry Street, Dublin. To boost take-up by prospective female patients, one testimonial boasts 'lady in constant attendance'. Consultations were free and 'charges most moderate', with 'dentists at 5 to 10 guineas'. Another Dublin surgery (same edition) advertises fillings at 2s 6d, extractions 1s 6d and sets of false teeth from 40s.

LEISURE AND RECREATION

An affluent woman's life was a comfortable one. She oversaw her servants who executed the hard graft, although many employed a butler and housekeeper to fulfil even this role. She might have minimal engagement with her children supervised by nanny in the nursery, sons despatched to boarding school at any age from 5 and daughters in the schoolroom with the governess.

Freed from responsibility, these women could indulge accomplishments: drawing, singing, playing the piano and visiting friends. Following the invention of the sewing machine, she could even take up Mrs Beeton's suggestion of wives and mothers sewing children's clothes as a labour of love.

Until the 1850s, the only acceptable physical exercise open to affluent women (virtually exclusive to them) was dancing and riding; no surprise then at the presence of dancing tutors in girls' schools. A fun explanation of etiquette at balls can be found in *The Modern Dancing Master* (1822) at *www.bl.uk/collection-items/the-modern-dancing-master*.

Archery was suitably decorous as described in Elizabeth Anne Galton's (1808–1906) memoirs *www.leamingtonhistory.co.uk /elizabeth-anne-galton-1808-1906*. Her diaries, letters and other ephemera cover diverse and wide-ranging topics, treatment for women's ailments, day-to-day recreation, 'coming out', visiting friends and relations (eating at 5.30 p.m. was 'very late'). The Galton Papers are in the University College London archives *http://archives. ucl.ac.uk* with extracts, family trees and photographs in descendant Andrew Moilliet's book, *Elizabeth Anne Galton (1808–1906): A Well Connected Gentlewoman*, Léonie Press, 2003.

If women wanted to follow the hunt before the 1830s, they took a carriage on lanes and roads rather than ride cross-country – both dangerous and unseemly. It took Frenchman Jules Pellier's invention of the side-saddle jumping pommel before women could ride to hounds i.e. fox hunt.

The International Horse Show (now Royal International Horse Show), the oldest horse show in the UK, was first held at Olympia in 1907 and immediately included in the social calendar betwixt Epsom and Ascot. Reserved seats cost from 2s 6d. Only a handful of women exhibited or competed here, prize winners (and mishaps) were published in contemporary newspapers.

Postcard advertising the International Horse Show 5–15 June 1909, Olympia. Author's collection © Adèle Emm

Postcard reverse International Horse show. Author's collection © Adèle Emm

International Horse Show
OLYMPIA, LONDON.
June 5th to 15th, 1909 (The week between Epsom and Ascot.)

OFFICES: - - - 12. Hanover Square, London, W.

Girls' schools perceived cricket as an appropriate activity and it was played from the 1770s (an English School painting depicts the Countess of Derby playing at Marylebone Cricket Club). Disputed cricketing folklore claims overarm bowling was innovated by

Christiana Willes (1786–1873). Hampered by her skirts bowling underarm to her brother John, she bowled overarm instead. Although the Women's Cricket Association was founded as late as 1926, the first women's cricket club, the White Heather Club, was founded in Yorkshire (where else?) in 1887.

The invention of the safety bicycle (1890s) brought independence to progressive and daring women who could afford the initial cost. At first, such middle-class women were satirised by humourists and illustrators, especially if wearing trousers to pursue her new craze. By the early twentieth century, the sheer practicality of the bicycle had widened its appeal.

A history of women's cycling is at *www.sheilahanlon.com/?p= 1889.* American devotee Maria E Ward's 1896 *Cycling for Ladies,* *https://archive.org/details/commonsensebicy00wardgoog* is a fabulous contemporary view of the activity.

Newspapers responded to its popularity by publishing advice to 'wheelwomen'. The *Sligo Champion*, 21 August 1897, wrote a list of patronising don'ts: 'don't ride without gloves; don't wear flaming colours in your hat; don't allow your escort to ride inside, nearest the sidewalk. That is your place . . . Don't make short turns at corners . . . Don't keep on ringing your bell when you see that the driver of a horse is turning out to make room for you . . .' Elsewhere, cycling was proposed as good for health, improving circulation and 'increased digestive power'. Critics were censorious of 'reckless' wheelwomen who 'never used brakes'.

The majority of reported accidental deaths were for working-class men (riding recklessly?) but there were inevitable female tragedies. Major's daughter, Evelyn Alice Carleton from Tiverton, 24, died of lockjaw in 1896 (curable today) a week after breaking her leg falling off her bicycle. In Park Street, Grosvenor Square, London, July 1895, widow Laura M. Campbell, 42, died from 'over exertion', although on re-examination it was blood poisoning following an illegal operation. The newspaper was reticent; was this an abortion?

Cycling clubs proliferated countrywide including the Lady Cyclists' Association (LCA). Enlightened clubs such as the Clarion

Cycling Club (*https://clarioncc.org*, founded 1894 and still in existence) admitted women from the start – the Clarion had socialist leanings. Manchester Lady Cyclists was founded 1898, and London had clubs in e.g. Brixton, Clapham and Kensington. Nursing aficionados could belong to Guys Hospital Nurses' Cycling Association.

Surviving bicycling club records are found locally. Try TNA first. The Modern Records Centre at Warwick University lists locations for resources from 1878 including a webpage on the Cyclists Touring Club plus links; *http://mrc-catalogue.warwick.ac.uk/records/CTC*. There is limited information on women per se.

The University of Cardiff's project, Women in Trousers: A Visual Archive *www.womenintrousers.org*, features contemporary illustrations of female *gens bracata* (people in trousers) as daring fashion statement, for work and sporting participation.

From the end of the nineteenth century, cars for the ultra-rich became popular although few women dared take the wheel (driving licences became law in 1903; the driving test mandatory from 1934). In 1901, Consuelo Vanderbilt, wife of the 9th Duke of Marlborough, was given a Waverley, an American electric car marketed towards women for its cleanliness. In 1908, a 6 horse power Rover with hood and glass screen cost between £105 and £150 – a clerk's annual salary.

Shopping as a leisure activity was an indulgence for the middle and higher classes; working-class women had limited time and money. Before the 1840s and 1850s, as explained by Elizabeth Anne Galton, shops were functional with little variety; a draper, general store and weekly or bi-weekly market sufficed for an entire town or village. After the introduction of the department store from the 1860s (Chapter 5), fashionable women undertook shopping excursions and, under the entry 'Ladies Shopping', *Dickens' Dictionary of London*, 1882, suggested suitable restaurants where unaccompanied ladies could lunch. He particularly recommended Verney's Restaurant, Regent Street, an interesting location at a time when Regent Street was notorious at night (Chapter 3).

Towards the end of the nineteenth century, women's clubs

proliferated for the privileged and well educated. Somerville was founded in 1878, The University Women's Club, Mayfair *www. universitywomensclub.com* in 1883 by Gertrude Jackson of Girton College, Cambridge. Many others offered amenities like lectures, lodgings in London and elsewhere to kindred spirits; see *https://womanandhersphere.com/2012/11/16/rooms-of-their-own-victorian -and-edwardian-womens-clubs-a-practical-demand.*

Music, Music Halls and Theatre

Respectable women didn't attend the theatre alone or even with a group of women. Unless she accompanied her husband or father, she could be assumed a prostitute. Tickets for the Theatre Royal, Covent Garden, 1841, had boxes at 7s and 5s; the pit cost 3s and the gallery 1s. Escorted by her beau, a working-class girl might sit in the cheapest seats; the affluent purchased a box or seat in the Grand Circle. Boxes at the Haymarket Theatre were cheaper at 5s; pit 3s and galleries 1s–2s. Suburban and provincial theatres were better value. The directory *A Swell's Night Guide*, 1841, listed which London theatres had rooms for a risqué rendezvous.

Offering a variety of delights, music hall was popular from the 1850s. According to the *Directory of London*, 1882, acts featured performing animals, Channel swimmers, conjurors, ventriloquists, campanologists, sword swallowers, illuminated fountains and orchestras *militaires*. Evidently not a fan, Dickens commented, 'Surely a dramatic entertainment even of a humble kind is better for the moral well-being of the audience of music halls, than the silly and too often indecent songs of most of the so-called comic singers.' Performances began around 8 p.m., ending at 11.30, cost of admission between 6d to 3s but private rooms pricier.

Middle- and upper-class women did not generally frequent music hall although, with predictably double standards, stage door johnnies might be from any class. Lower class women did go. Eliza Southey visited one with her soldier boyfriend in Dover, 1882, with disastrous consequences (Chapter 3). For those working in theatre and music hall, see Chapter 5.

The responsibility for so few ladies' lavatories in Victorian theatres rests on the 1875 Public Health Act when it was 'improper' for women to use public facilities. Queues persist today.

Etiquette

Missionary's wife Mrs Sarah Stickney Ellis (1799–1872) published *The Women of England, Their Social Duties and Domestic Habits* in 1839 (*https://archive.org/details/womenofenglandth00ellirich*). Targeted at young wives 'who belong to that great mass of population of England which is connected with trade and manufacture, as well as to wives and daughters of professional men of limited incomes', her books were intended to inspire middle-class women to harness religious duty and improve society by first improving themselves.

The book covered chapters on education, dress, manners, conversation, domestic habits, consideration and kindness, love, public opinion, monetary resources and integrity. Ellis espoused kindness and consideration towards servants and others; high moral principles rather than an extensive academic education. Women should read improving books rather than learn Latin and walk in meadows studying botany and flowers in order to contribute to polite conversation. A girl's voice, she maintained, should be melodious and well-regulated, and if a husband is of 'moody temperament' she should 'ply her needle' and 'sit quietly musing'.

Spinsters

Mrs Ellis was aware of the difficult position in which an unmarried woman found herself. Despised and pitied by married sisters, she reminds her readers that a spinster or maiden aunt had been accustomed to a higher standard of living when younger. Once her father had died, a spinster 'in the middle rank' survived on the good will of brother, distant uncle or friends – universally regarded as a burden.

Her description of these unfortunates was that they slept in a whitewashed attic in a small single bed spurned by the daughters in the family. She justified her keep by replacing and sewing back missing buttons, finding ribbons, mending linen and darning household socks and stockings. Ellis' message was that her married sisters should be charitable, generous and loving towards these 'appendages'. It could be them . . .

Libraries

As directed by Mrs Ellis, if a woman was to improve herself, she needed access to books. Libraries (also known as circulating libraries) were subscription based until the Public Libraries Act, 1850, entitling boroughs to establish free ones. In the face of fierce opposition (increased taxation, the promotion of social unrest and questioning the necessity when so few could read), only towns with a population of more than 10,000 were permitted to offer this free service. The first, 1852, opened its doors in Manchester. In 1853, the Act was extended to Scotland.

Offering less chance of mingling with the hoi polloi, the more prosperous still patronised subscription libraries rather than free ones. *Dickens Dictionary of London* lists circulating libraries plus terms and conditions, e.g. books could not be changed more than once a day. London appears to have been better value than Henry Lovett's Library, Bognor Regis. A Victorian media mogul capitalising on holidaymakers as well as residents, Lovett advertised his rates in his newspaper, *Bognor Regis Advertiser*, 2 January 1878. A set of books (one novel in three volumes) borrowed for a week cost 1s 6d; 2s 6d for two sets of books for a fortnight. To use his reading room, a year's subscription for one cost £25; £40 for a family. To borrow books and frequent his reading room, an individual paid a hefty annual subscription of £35, £60 for a family – well out of reach of the working-class whose annual household incomes were often well below this figure.

Rise of holidays

For the aristocracy, 'the grand tour' was popular from the late eighteenth century. Following the advent of the railway in the 1840s, travel was easier, faster and more comfortable and such excursions percolated down to the middle classes. *Little Women* (1868/1869) and *What Katy Did Next* (1886) by American writers Louisa May Alcott and Susan Coolidge feature young women taken as companions on European tours. E M Forster's novel *A Room with a View* (1908) depicted Lucy Honeychurch's adventures in Italy. For the lucky few, family souvenirs, diaries and letters may survive.

Foreign travel required a passport. The Foreign Office Passport Office Registers Index 1851–1916 (ref FO611) is available to download (free) as part of the Digital Microfilm Project at the TNA see *www.nationalarchives.gov.uk/help-with-your-research/research-guides/free-online-records-digital-microfilm*, instructions on the website. Scroll through passport holders to find serial number and

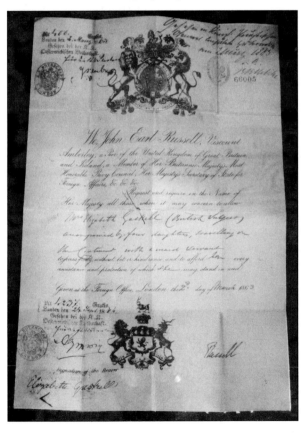

Elizabeth Gaskell's passport dated 2 March 1863. Courtesy Elizabeth Gaskell's House, Manchester.

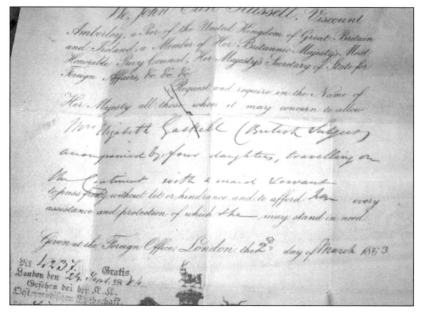

Passport detail offering safe passage for Elizabeth Gaskell, four daughters and female servant. Courtesy Elizabeth Gaskell's House, Manchester.

date of issue. These are under years, e.g. 1851, 1852 and there's no index for 1863–73.

Dated 2 March 1863, writer Elizabeth Gaskell's (1810–65) passport is displayed in her Manchester home *http://elizabeth gaskellhouse.co.uk.* It was also valid for four (unnamed) daughters and (unnamed) maidservant.

However, most women toured England rather than Europe; in *Pride and Prejudice*, fictional Elizabeth Bennett visited Derbyshire with her uncle and aunt.

By the early twentieth century, even the working class took short holidays, preferably by the seaside. Although swimming costumes were featured in women's journals from the 1860s, sea bathing achieved mass popularity later in the century, celebrated on the postcard.

Plain postcards developed from 1870, picture postcards available from 1894; their golden age between 1900 and 1907. From 1902,

THE GOOD OLD SUMMER TIME

THE MERMAID

'The Mermaid' posted 19 June 1905. Author's collection © Adèle Emm

message and address were written on the same side and an illustration, photo or humorous cartoon, printed on the reverse. With several deliveries a day, one posted in the morning announcing safe arrival was received at its destination that afternoon. My family are hoarders so I'm lucky enough to have inherited a collection illustrating places and activities that ancestors, friends and family enjoyed, including the Royal Parade, Eastbourne, sent to Mrs Lomas of Birmingham (a distant relative?). Dated 1905, it shows holidaying middle-class Edwardian women sauntering along the promenade sheltering from the sun with parasols; freckles and sun tan were anathema to the middle and upper class.

Nonconformist employers such as chocolate manufacturers Cadbury and Rowntree were amongst the first to appreciate a healthy, contented workforce was more productive and from the 1850s provided workers and their families holidays by the sea. Most were unpaid (paid holidays were legalised in 1938) but a handful of firms, Rowntree for instance, chartered a train and covered the fare. Some factories administered holiday savings clubs. There are few surviving records and many archives are not open to the public.

Eastbourne postcard, 1905. Author's collection © Adèle Emm

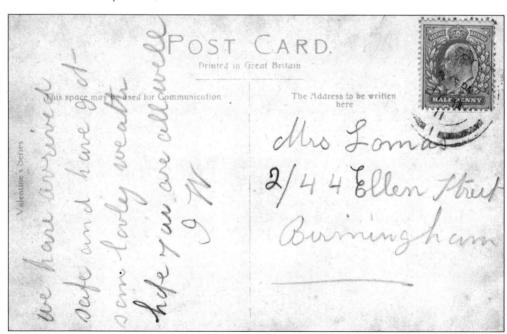

'Arrived safely.' Reverse, Eastbourne postcard, 1905. Author's collection © Adèle Emm

Rowntree's, now part of Nestlé, are held at the Borthwick Institute but not generally available.

COST OF LIVING

It's interesting to compare the cost of living today with that of the past. One comparison site is the Bank of England's *www.bank ofengland.co.uk/monetary-policy/inflation* calculating inflation (at the time of writing) from 1209 to 2016. An alternative site *www. whatsthecost.com/cpi.aspx* calculates from 1751. Its page on *www. whatsthecost.com/historic.cpi.aspx* gives annual interest rates although, as it points out, the CPI (Consumer Price Index) didn't exist before 1996 so earlier rates are speculative and unofficial.

Depending on which of these two websites you use, an annual rent of £10 in 1867 (when a householder paid Poor Law taxes) would be £1,010 today. A middle-class family's income of £200 a year in 1867 would equate to about £20,000. Of course, buying power was much higher than today.

MAPS

For those with London ancestors, Charles Booth's *Maps Descriptive of London Poverty* from his *Inquiry into Life and Labour in London 1886–1903* give a graphic economic description of roads and streets in the metropolis. Socialist and social reformer Beatrice Webb née Potter (1858–1943) was a volunteer on this project. The originals can be consulted in the Society of Genealogists or viewed online at *https://booth.lse.ac.uk/map.*

Booth used seven colour classifications of poverty:

- black – lowest class: vicious. semi-criminal
- dark blue – very poor: casual. chronic want
- light blue – poor: 18s to 21s a week for a moderate family
- purple – mixed: some comfortable, others poor
- pink – fairly comfortable: good ordinary earnings
- red – middle class: well to do
- yellow – upper middle and upper classes: wealthy

Two colours meant a mixture of socio-economic classes. Armed with the census address of your female ancestor, you can consult the London maps and relate economic status to where she lived.

MARIO *http://mario.lancashire.gov.uk/agsmario* (Maps and Related Information Online) is administered by Lancashire County Council and enables users to compare old maps with current topology. By clicking on an area, historical maps are superimposed on today's. MARIO includes parts of Yorkshire 'moved' to Lancashire, 1974.

Other historic maps can be found at *www.british-history.ac.uk/ catalogue/maps, www.old-maps.co.uk* or *www.oldmapsonline.org,* often linking through to the National Library of Scotland's *http://maps.nls.uk* online resource – another excellent free site. Manchester University's LUNA project has historical Manchester maps from 1794 at *www. library.manchester.ac.uk/search-resources/special-collections/guide-to- special-collections/map-collection/online-map-collection.* Some libraries allow readers to view originals.

The Lloyd George Domesday Survey, 1910, is on TheGenealogist (subscription) and useful for roads which have disappeared, e.g. due to the London Blitz, regeneration, renumbering of houses, etc. It matches an ancestor's house on large-scale hand-annotated maps of London (5 feet to the inch) plotting the exact property in 1910. Fully searchable by name, the map is revealed on one icon and accompanying field books which include occupier, owner, situation and description on another. An example is Mrs Jane Linton of 120 Shirland Road, Maida Vale; the house was owned by Welford & Sons of 97 Elgin Avenue, its rateable value was £40. Click on the map icon to reveal she neighbours Warwick Farm Dairy. Elgin Avenue, her landlord's address, is just around the corner. In 1911, Jane, 59, mother to two surviving children, is a widowed professor of music living in three rooms. Her visitor was a 54-year-old married Italian, also professor of music.

PHOTOGRAPHS
My mother asked my grandfather to name everyone in our family

albums for which I am eternally grateful. Your children may not know Great Uncle Fred, so please do this now.

One of the largest photographic collections is that of Francis Frith (1822–98) and his myriad photographers. Travelling the country with a camera, they recorded what they saw, often just views but occasionally people conducting their daily life. Many coffee-table books have been published from the collection and the archive is online *www.francisfrith.com/uk.*

It's unusual for featured people to be named unless famous. Local newspapers may subtitle photographs but printing techniques weren't as sophisticated as today and there are few photographs of ordinary people in newspapers prior to 1914.

Libraries and CROs hold photographic collections. Some can be searched online but others have not been fully catalogued. Don't expect to find characters named unless they were significant – a headmistress, superintendent of an industrial school, councillor etc.

Although produced from the tail end of the nineteenth century, you're unlikely to find useful films or moving images prior to 1900. The BFI *http://www.bfi.org.uk* is amongst the largest film collections in the world and the North West Film Archive *www.nwfa.mmu. ac.uk/about.htm* holds pioneering general views from the very late 1890s.

Bibliography and Further Reading

Baker, Richard Anthony, *British Music Hall: An Illustrated History*, Pen & Sword, 2014

Barratt, Nick, *Tracing the History of Your House: The Building, the People, the Past* , PRO, 2006

Blanchard, Gill, *Tracing Your House History*, Pen & Sword, 2013

Clarke, William Spencer, *The Suburban Homes of London: A Residential Guide*, Chatto & Windus, 1881, online *https://archive. org/stream/suburbanhomeslo00clargoog#page/n10/mode/2up*

Ellis, Sarah Stickney, *The Women of England, their Social Duties &c &c*, Fisher, Son & Co., London, 1839

Engels, Friedrich, *The Condition of the Working Class in England*,

1845; trans. from German by Florence Kelley Wischnewetzky, William Reeves, 1888

Flanders, Judith, *The Victorian House*, Harper Collins, 2003

Hughes, Kathryn, *Short Life and Long Times of Mrs Beeton*, Harper, 2006

Hannavy, John, *The Victorian and Edwardian Tourist*, Bloomsbury Shire, 2012

Matthews, Neil, *Victorians and Edwardians Abroad, The Beginning of the Modern Holiday*, Pen & Sword, 2016

Moilliet, Andrew, ed., *Elizabeth Anne Galton (1808–1906): A Well Connected Gentlewoman*, Léonie Press, 2003

Newby, Jennifer, *Women's Lives, Researching Women's Social History, 1800–1939*, Pen & Sword, 2011

O'Neill, Joseph, *The Secret World of the Victorian Lodging House,* Pen & Sword, 2014

Roberts, Elizabeth, *A Woman's Place: An Oral History of Working-Class Women, 1890–1940,* Blackwell, 1984

Stobart, Jon, *Spend Spend Spend: A History of Shopping,* History Press, 2008

Upton, Chris, *Living Back to Back,* Phillimore, 2005

Ward, Maria E, *Bicycling for Ladies,* Brentano's New York, 1896
https://archive.org/details/commonsensebicy00wardgoog

Yorke, Trevor, *The Victorian House Explained,* Countryside Books, 2005

Chapter 5

A HARD DAY'S WORK

Betsy Waring (who goes out a-charing)
is a Martyr to Rheumatics
(what comes o' damp attics).
(*Punch*, 6 February 1876)

Affluent women did not have paid occupations although those with a social conscience might champion philanthropic causes. Clergyman's wife, feminist and social reformer Josephine Butler (1828–1906) was ostracised for fighting for the rights of prostitutes (Chapter 3). Self-taught social reformer, historian and socialist, Beatrice Webb née Potter (1858–1943) co-founded the London School of Economics. A few notable women wrote; Mrs Gaskell (another clergyman's wife), Mrs Beeton, and, writing under her husband's name Mrs Linnaeus Banks, Isabella née Varley. For twenty years, Irish writer and battered wife, Margaret Gardiner, Countess of Blessington, (née Power, 1789–1849) reputedly made £2,000 a year producing novels, poetry and travelogues.

A reason for publishing under *Mrs* or hiding behind a male pseudonym like George Eliot (Mary Anne Evans), and Currer, Acton and Ellis Bell (the Brontës) was to avoid public disapprobation and maintain a smattering of respectability. When budding author and poet Charlotte Brontë (1816–55) sent poems to Robert Southey in 1837 for advice, she received the following reply: 'Literature cannot be the business of a woman's life, and it ought not to be. The more she is engaged in her proper duties, the less leisure will she have for it even as an accomplishment and a recreation.' The letter is at the Bronte Parsonage Museum, Haworth *www.bronte.org.uk.*

The first (anti) science fiction novel, Mary Shelley's *Frankenstein* (1818) was published anonymously and, during her lifetime, Jane Austen's novels were 'by A Lady'. In 1852, not wanting to overshadow her esteemed husband Charles at the height of his fame, Catherine Dickens published a 'bill of fare' cookbook, *What Shall We Have for Dinner*, under pseudonym Maria Clutterbuck; available online, it makes fascinating reading.

Life for the middle classes was a tenuous balance between prosperity and penury, and it was frighteningly easy to slide from one to the other. Profligacy, sickness or death of a husband potentially tipped a middle-class family into crisis. For women unaccustomed and ill-equipped to work through lack of education, skills or training, she must pay the rent any way she could. In E Nesbit's *The Railway Children* (1905/6), it was the father's false imprisonment which triggered their catastrophe. In this fictional example, the family decamped from London to a cheaper location, Yorkshire, where mother wrote short stories to survive. In reality, many scraped by with needlework skills; girls learned to sew as a child (surviving samplers are treasured family mementos). A middle-class mother supporting her family couldn't go into service – what middle-class woman would take her? She had neither subservience nor practical skills. Following the sudden death of her father, the middle-class heroine of Thomas Hardy's *Desperate Remedies* (1871) unsuccessfully advertised herself as maid, becoming a companion instead. And, because she wasn't sufficiently educated, a widow was unlikely to gain a position as governess, although a few opened small private schools for girls concentrating on pupils acquiring accomplishments – usually for a supplement. At all costs, families from every class battled against the workhouse's beckoning finger.

It's unusual to find a middle-class woman state her occupation in a census (Elizabeth Gaskell is wife, 1861) but a working-class woman frequently did. In many northern cities the percentage of working women was extraordinarily high; 70 per cent of employees in Dundee's jute industry in 1901 were women. As many women were expected to give up work when they married, this is an

Elizabeth Gaskell's House, Manchester. writer Elizabeth Gaskell was enumerated as 'wife' when she lived here 1850–65. © Adèle Emm

extraordinary statistic. Other women recorded themselves in censuses as 'farmer's wife' or 'baker's wife', clearly proud of the association with their husband and presumably involved in the business.

Before the first genealogically useful census of 1841, it's difficult to discover what work, if any, a female ancestor was engaged in so we must make assumptions that, if she did work, it was as servant, mill-hand, on the land, cottage industry or assisting her husband.

To further obfuscate the issue, the 1841 census didn't publish specific categories for wives and children's occupations, therefore an enumerator wasn't obliged to declare a part-time or casual job. He was also disinclined to record a woman working in an illegal or unsavoury venture such as prostitution. Furthermore, according to a 1999 article by Matthew Woollard of University of Essex Historical Censuses and Social Surveys Research Group, even terms 'Help at

Home', 'Home Work' and 'Household Duties' are potentially misleading when women described thus could be domestic servants or wives running a household. To summarise, although a woman was recorded as having no 'rank, possession or occupation', she may have had paid work, however menial, contributing a few pence to family finance.

Some occupations metamorphosed due to technological advance; factories are the prime example. Nine female ostrich feather cleaners worked in London in 1871. By 1881 and 1891, there were two or three men cleaning and dyeing feathers but the majority were women, a handful toiling outside the capital. Fashion is fickle and this industry failed spectacularly at the turn of the nineteenth/ twentieth century, a casualty combination from the rise of the car (ostrich feathers were too large to fit in or ravaged by the wind) and austerity of the First World War when flaunting extravagant hats was considered inappropriate.

Other jobs were specific to women: charwoman, laundress, maid, nurse. The female secretary is a twentieth-century phenomenon, although there were a handful of 'lady typewriters' and 'shorthand clerks' from the 1890s. However, the thousands of clerks beavering away at accounts, official legal documents and copying letters were men. In 1911, 478 female clerical workers were recorded in the census, none in some earlier ones.

LABOUR LAWS

In the late 1790s, Richard Arkwright's female and child labour at Cromford Mill, Derbyshire, worked two shifts over a twenty-four hour day; the cost of lighting offset against his profits. Arkwright was considered a benevolent employer who provided good housing for workers.

From the early nineteenth century social reformers, appalled at the conditions they saw, attempted to improve the lot of working women and children. In 1819, the Cotton Mills and Factory Act, the first of many, attempted to restrict working hours for women and children. It became illegal to employ children under 9 and limited working hours to sixteen a day for anyone under 16. Because it failed to include provision for enforcement, mill owners largely ignored it.

However, the 1833 Factory Act regulating cotton, wool, linen/flax and silk industries (omitted from previous legislation) ensured compliance by engaging four male inspectors to enforce the compulsory two hours a day schooling of children under 13. It was also obligatory to employ doctors to verify child employees' age which, because many children didn't know, was calculated by height; the taller, the older.

Until the 1842 Mines and Collieries Act, women and children worked underground eleven or twelve hours a day earning less than their menfolk. This Act banned females and boys under 10 from working underground. The *UK Commissioners Report of Children's Employment*, 1842, instrumental in ratifying this Act, is on Ancestry at *https://search.ancestry.co.uk/search/db.aspx?dbid=34775*. Its often shocking evidence consisting of 877 pages names women and children, their working conditions and pay in a variety of heavy industries in Ireland, Scotland, Wales and England. For photographs of Wigan female surface colliery workers at the turn of the twentieth century to the 1940s see *www.wiganworld.co. uk/album/showalbum.php?offset=0&opt=3&gallery=Colliery+Lasses +%2F+Pit+Brow+Girls*.

The 1844 Factory Act restricted women and young people under 18 from working nights and to a twelve-hour day with a one and a half hour meal break. Bearing in mind meal breaks were unpaid, women were still on factory premises for thirteen and a half hours a day. This was the first Act legislating on safety; dangerous machinery was fenced off. However, everything is relative; what is considered dangerous today may not have been in 1844.

It took a ten-year campaign to pass the hotly contested but well-intentioned 1847 Ten Hour Act. With fewer working hours, many were concerned it might further reduce employees' wages. With women and children restricted to a ten-hour working day, eight-hour Saturday and Sundays off, the working week was officially a maximum fifty-eight hours. Not so. With no inspectors to ensure compliance, unscrupulous factory owners ignored it.

There was no such legislation for shop assistants, servants and seamstresses. Seamstresses could, and often did, work overnight if dresses were required for the London season – when Parliament assembled between October (occasionally November) to May/June, the summer recess. During these months, expensive, elaborate costumes were required at short notice by wealthy families attending parties and social events to introduce unmarried daughters to eligible, influential and preferably affluent prospective husbands.

By 1867, under Factory Acts (Extension) legislation, women and children in all factories were restricted to a twelve-hour day and finished at 2 pm on Saturdays. As ever, it was difficult to enforce. The ten-hour working day for women and children was finally achieved in 1874.

TRADE UNIONS AND STRIKES

Although it's more likely men belonged to a trade union simply because they worked in higher skilled jobs, there are examples of women joining and striking for better conditions and pay. The most famous example is the Bryant & May match girls strike, summer 1888. Not only were these girls (many very young) paid appalling wages whilst the company made huge profits, they were also badly disfigured by phosphorous poisoning.

In a nutshell; after three colleagues had been dismissed from the Bow factory several girls made a deputation to socialist and activist Annie Besant (1847–1933) who embraced their cause. Publishing a diatribe in her weekly agit-prop journal, *The Link, A Journal for the Servants of Man*, she compared Bryant & May to the white slave trade.

More than 1,100 girls went on a strike lasting over three weeks. The inaugural meeting of the Union of Women Match Makers, 27 July 1888, was delivered by Clementina Black of the Women's Trade Union League who advised on rules, subscriptions and elections. By October, there were more than 666 members. At the end of the year, its name was changed to the Matchmaker Union and open to both men and women. The Union closed in 1903. A new Bryant & May factory was built 1909–10 and by 1911, over 2,000 women were employed there. The site has since been redeveloped into a residential complex, the Bow Quarter.

Surviving copies of *The Link* are held at the British Library with some editions online. Contemporary newspapers contain considerable information about the match girls' strike; see the BNA. You're unlikely to discover if an ancestor was a striker but any woman living in Bow enumerated in 1881/1891 censuses as 'matchmaker' or 'employed at match factory' may well have worked for Bryant & May. One hopes those enumerated in 1891 saw improved conditions . . .

There were several influential female trade unionists beside Annie Besant and Clementina Black. Scottish born suffragist and trade unionist Mary Reid Macarthur (1880–1921; she married William Anderson in 1911) is commemorated by a blue plaque at 42 Woodstock Road, Golders Green *www.english-heritage.org.uk/visit/blue-plaques/macarthur-mary-1880-1921.* A statue in Mary Macarthur Gardens, Cradley Heath, Staffordshire, honours her involvement in the ten-week 1910 strike when female chain workers demanded a minimum wage and implementation. She helped form the National Federation of Women Workers (1909), the National Anti-Sweating League (against sweat shops, 1906), Women's Trade Union League and founded the journal *Woman Worker* in 1907.

A website for industrial relations (or not) is the Trade Union's Congress (TUC) at *www.unionhistory.info.* Also see *www.union ancestors.co.uk* or *www.wcml.org.uk/our-collections/working-lives.* FindMyPast has British Trade Union Membership Registers. Trade Unions records from 1846 are held at Warwick University in the Modern Records Centre *www2.warwick.ac.uk/services/library/mrc.*

The People's History Museum, Manchester, is worth visiting *www.phm.org.uk.* It holds the Labour History Archive and Study Centre where archives including the Women's Labour League collection for 1906–18 provide an insight into social, political and economic life of the past two centuries. The Working Class Movement Library, Salford, *www.wcml.org.uk,* is another specialist centre.

Newspapers and journals which covered trade unions (not necessarily women's issues) include: *The Bee-Hive* (1861–78), *Economic Journal* (from 1891), *Cotton Factory Times* (1885–1937), *Women's Trade Union Review* (held at TUC Library Collection) and *The Clarion* (from 1891 with a women's column virtually from conception).

Bibliography and Further Reading

Beer, Reg, *Matchgirls Strike 1888: The Struggle Against Sweated Labour in London's East End*, National Museum of Labour History, 1979

Boston, Sarah, *Women Workers and the Trade Unions*, Lawrence & Wishart, 2015

Crail, Mark, *Tracing Your Labour Movement Ancestors*, Pen & Sword, 2009

Drake, Barbara, *Women in Trade Unions*, Virago, 1984

Lewenhak, Sheila, *Women and Trade Unions*, Ernest Benn, 1977

May, Trevor, *Victorian Factory Life*, Bloomsbury Shire, 2011

Soldon, Norbert C, *Women in British Trade Unions, 1874–1976*, Gill & Macmillan, 1978

Stafford, Ann, *A Match to Fire the Thames*, Hodder & Stoughton, 1961

FINDING EMPLOYMENT

It never ceases to amaze me how far people travelled to find work; country to country, rural areas to towns and cities. From the 1760s into the 1850s, landowners in Scotland cleared the Highlands. Fleeing poverty and famine, the Irish landed in Liverpool in the mid-nineteenth century. Huge numbers escaped religious intolerance in Europe and arrived in the UK. People either stayed where they fetched up or sought their fortune elsewhere.

Housemaids at Blenheim Palace in 1851 originated from local

Woodstock but also from Norfolk, Suffolk and Surrey. At Lyme Hall, Cheshire, 1861, the housekeeper, Elizabeth Gibson (39, unmarried), hailed from Golspie, north Scotland, a lady's maid was from Leicestershire and two nursemaids from Flintshire, Wales.

Once someone arrived in a new area, how did they find a job? Potential employers placed advertisements in newspapers and magazines; this is how fictional Jane Eyre found her governess role at Thornfield Hall but it was a well-established method; after all, to work as a governess, women had to be educated enough to write a creditable letter of application. Governesses often advertised themselves in *The Times*.

Poaching staff from friends and neighbours was not unusual (destined to evoke animosity?) especially if an acquaintance had a celebrated cook or efficient housekeeper. The landed gentry wouldn't hobnob in servants' quarters of another house, but clandestine servant-to-servant enquiries could be made.

Word of mouth was another failsafe way of finding employment. If a business needed hands, they asked around the neighbourhood. For family concerns like shops and bakeries, of course, a daughter helped out. My great grandmother was an assistant at her father's bakery, later becoming a cook in service.

Front pages of newspapers held, alongside headlines, advertisements for commercial enterprises such as shop and house sales. Some newspapers placed *situations vacant* and *wanted* here but cheaper advertisements were on the inside. Page 4 of *The Leeds Intelligencer*, 5 December 1846, ran an advert 'Housemaid. A respectable young woman with satisfactory recommendations from her last situation. Apply to the printers.'

A woman could place an advertisement herself; 'Wanted, by a Young Woman, a situation as Upper Housemaid, or housemaid in a small family where a footman is kept. Can have a good character from her last situation. Apply (if by letter pre-paid) to R Pollden, linen-draper, Market Square, Aylesbury,' *The Bucks Herald*, 14 November 1840.

In 1895, it cost 6d for twenty words prepaid to place a personal advertisement in *The Buckingham Advertiser and Press*. Employers advertising vacancies were charged 1s for twenty words prepaid, 1s 6d if booked.

Employment agencies are not a twentieth-century phenomenon; Elizabeth Raffald (1733–81) opened a servants' agency in Manchester in the late eighteenth century. Another, the Domestic Bazaar in Oxford Street, London (formerly The Agency established 1830), routinely placed advertisements in newspapers. Page 4 of the *Morning Advertiser*, 29 June 1832, offered '30 or 40 vacant situations for females and males', promising families 'respectable servants with good characters'. The agency charged employers. There was 'no charge made to servants of All-work' when appealing for waitresses, female servants for a coffee house and cook in the *Morning Advertiser*, 11 April 1834.

For those intending to relocate to another part of the country, local papers usually had head offices in London, making it feasible to advertise jobs in counties some distance from its demographic readership.

APPRENTICES

Just like men, women took apprenticeships especially in trades like dressmaker, seamstress and milliner, but they were also apprenticed to factories. Textile mills employed agents to travel the country from parish to parish touting for potential employees via Poor Law Guardians. Mill owners preferred employing girls who were deemed less troublesome and more tractable than boys. Another advantage was, should they be taken on at the end of an apprenticeship, they were paid less than men. Country-bred children, taller and with better health and stamina, were preferred over city children. Apprentices at Quarry Bank Mill, Cheshire, originated from as far south as Buckinghamshire.

People were paid to take on apprentices. In 1913, a two-year apprenticeship to a Manchester confectioner incurred a £10 indenture. In the 1840s, Quarry Bank Mill was paid two guineas (£2.10) by the Overseers of the Poor for each girl taken on.

It was a win-win situation for those paying Poor Law taxes. The employer removed children from expensive care, provided training (albeit for low-skilled jobs) and housed, clothed and fed them whilst profiting from often unpaid labour. Once adult, their trade ostensibly protected them from re-entering the workhouse. However, unscrupulous mill owners indulged in what would now be called human trafficking. In May 1852, eleven young girls, seduced by the promise of an education, high wages and short working hours, relocated from their home in Skye to work at Hollins Mill, Marple, Cheshire. As ever, if something appears too good to be true, it probably is. Life at Hollins Mill was so harsh one girl wrote home to complain and, beaten so badly, she died. Reverend John Forbes, their church minister in Skye, battled to get them home but they were stripped of clothing and refused money for the journey. The sad story of their ultimate return (two girls died shortly after arriving home) was recounted in newspapers including *Fife Herald*, 29 September 1853. Hollins Mill was not alone in its degrading and inhuman treatment of the workforce.

The quality of training and working conditions depended on the trade for which a child was apprenticed. In factories, many everywhere were poorly fed, faced dangerous machinery, high accident rates and routine beatings. Long hours were customary and, post-1833, compulsory schooling at the end of a tiring day.

Indenture records often do not survive. A copy was given to the parent/guardian and another kept by the master but, for illiterate parents, easily lost. Those that survive are held locally (not all have been catalogued) or within the family itself. Information on such records were; child's name, age, name of parent, date, trade for which the apprentice was being trained, pay and conditions attached such as holidays, uniform and tools. Some apprentice records, e.g. the Manchester Collection of Churchwarden and Overseers apprenticeship indentures for 1700–1913, have been digitised and found at *http://search.findmypast.co.uk/search-world-records/ manchester-apprentices.*

PAY

Women were paid less than men right into the twentieth century, hence, for instance, why so many more female mill hands than male. The Equal Pay Act is as recent as 1970. Promotion to management was unheard of. In a mill, the male overseer/overlooker supervised women in his domain, fining them for transgressions, for being late, not picking up dropped bobbins (1d each, Water-foot Mill, Haslingden, 1851). It also explains why, if she wanted to be master of her province with the potential of earning more, a widow continued a husband's business after his death.

Table 2. Sample rates of pay for men and women

job title – men	weekly wage
overseers and clerks, Halstead silk mill (HSM), 1825	15s–32s
mechanics and engine drivers, HSM	17s–25s
power loom attendants, HSM	14s–15s
mill machinery attendants and loom cleaners, HSM	10s–15s
spindle cleaners, packers, sweepers, HSM	5s–12s
mechanics, Quarry Bank Mill (QBM), cotton, 1831–50	18s–22s
carders, QBM	17s–18s
mule spinners, QBM	10s–13s
weavers, QBM	15s
weaver, Lancashire Mill, June 1870	16s +
male teacher, 1880	£50 p/a
job title – women	**weekly wage**
warpers, Halstead silk mill (HSM), 1825	7s–10s
twisters, HSM	7s–10s
wasters, HSM	6s–9s
weavers, HSM	5s–8s

drawers and doublers, HSM	4s–6s
winders, HSM	2s–4s
spinners, Quarry Bank Mill (QBM), cotton, 1831–50	6s 6d
reelers, QBM	5s–10s
throstle spinners, QBM	6s–7s
weavers, QBM	8s
weaver, Lancashire Mill, 1870	13s 5d
weaver, 3 looms, Hollins Mill, Lancashire, 1913	5s
mantua makers 1835; hours 9am-11pm daily	4s 8d
stay stitcher 1835	2s 6d
slop worker (cheap sweated clothing) 1835. at home (hours 7 a.m. to 12 midnight)	3s–9s
Edwardian dressmakers	10s
shop assistant, London department store, 1864 (includes board and lodging)	8s–£1
shop assistant aged 15, 1901 (local family-run business, includes board and lodging)	5s–6s
telegraphists, 1874	15s–30s
telephonists, 1901, at age 17	8s
apron machiner, East End sweat shop, 1913 (supplying own thread and light)	6s 3d
ironers, 1913	2d for 12 collars washed 6d for 144
school board headmistress, March 1874 (few women had the correct qualifications)	£124 rising to £200 p/a
female teacher 1880	£30 p/a

The following female occupations start with servants, the largest employer of women until the twentieth century; others follow alphabetically, plus suggested resources. Most require a trip to the CRO or TNA but, inevitably, some are online. This is not an exhaustive list, many women worked in their husband's business especially in small shops and I cannot include every female job enumerated in censuses. For professions, doctors, teachers, etc., see Chapter 6.

SERVANTS

In the 1851 census, 50 per cent of female employees in London were servants; in provincial cities, it was 40 per cent. They belonged to two types, live-in and live-out.

Those who lived-in received board and lodging plus uniform and therefore lower wages. They might receive one day off each week and perhaps a week's unpaid holiday a year. Those who lived-out were paid slightly more and, because hours were so long, might receive lunch. These were 'day servants'. Although some houses in my street, 1911, had live-in servants, a former resident remembers day servants arriving at six in the morning, having walked from home, and finishing late afternoon. Via steps at the rear of the house, she entered her cellar domain with copper, range and butler's stone sink. During the day, she made up fires, cleaned and dusted, laundered and ironed, cooked meals including breakfast, washed pots and answered the door to visitors and tradesmen. Out servants were enumerated at their home address and didn't necessarily work for one employer.

When the 1882 Select Committee for the Contagious Diseases Act (Chapter 3) examined Dover servant Eliza Southey, it gave an inadvertent and fascinating glimpse into a servant's life. For two years, Eliza had worked in service in Calais, the shortest period being nine months when she returned home ill. Although travelling to France in the late 1870s sounds (and was) adventurous for a working-class girl, the fastest ferry from Dover took a mere one and a half hours to cross the Channel (1854). Even today, a train journey from Dover to London takes just over an hour . . .

In Dover, she had a variety of jobs, routinely arriving home between 8 and 9 at night. Her working week was a drudgery of: Wednesdays, Mrs Souter in Hawksbury Street; Thursday to Saturday,

Mr Clout, an ironmonger and wife; once every six weeks, charring at Miss Molland's almshouse; Mondays and Tuesdays, unpaid cleaning for her 82-year-old unemployed mariner grandfather, Robert Southey, and bedridden aunt, Annie. This kind girl also helped her landlady, widow Sarah Ford, with mangling.

Live-in Servants

According to *Mrs Beeton's Book of Household Management* (first published 1861, frequently updated), a small household should engage three servants: a cook (doubling as housekeeper and supervising the other servants), a parlour maid and housemaid. In the morning, a live-out girl undertook heavy-duty cleaning and, if required, a fourth servant was the kitchen maid.

For £10 or less a year, any lower middle-class household where a husband earned £100 a year (a junior clerk, for instance) could afford a young maid-of-all-work, colloquially called the *skivvy* or *slavie*. Just as there was class delineation in society, so there was within the servant world. In a large establishment, the butler reigned supreme and, surprise surprise, male servants earned more than female.

Table 3. Rates of pay for servants

male servants (1825) and guineas p/a		female servants (1825) and guineas p/a	
French man-cook	80	housekeeper	24
butler	50	lady's maid	20
coachman	28	head nurse	20
footman	24	second nurse	10
under footman	20	nursery maid	7
lady's groom	12	upper house maid	15
		under house maid	14
		kitchen maid	14
		upper laundry maid	14

		under laundry maid	10
		dairy maid	8
		second maid	7
		still room maid	9
		scullion	9
Harewood House		lady's maid, 1874	£12 p/a
footman, 1892	£30 p/a	kitchen maid, 1892	£14 p/a
		skivvy live-in, suburbs	£10 p/a
		charwoman, live-out,	
		60 hours a week, 1860	9s p/w,
			plus beer, tea
			and sugar

The top part of this table draws from The Complete Servant by Samuel and Sarah Adams. This book was written by former servants so rates are artificially high. Compare with rates of pay at Harewood House in 1892, shown in the lower part of the table (*https:// servants.harewood.org*).

Elsewhere, the housekeeper and cook held the highest status, a charwoman the lowest. Each had clearly defined roles. Mrs Beeton explained that the housekeeper, who represented the head of the household, should be well-versed in accounts, keeping 'an accurate registry of all sums paid for any and every purpose, all the current expenses of the house, tradesmen's bills, and other extraneous matter'. In a large establishment, her room was where lower servants prepared meals and ate.

A housekeeper's life could be more exciting than you imagine. Eliza Jane Emm, born 1874 in a working-class Paddington family, progressed from milliner's assistant, servant in a Shepherd's Bush boarding house to fully blown housekeeper travelling to Durban, South Africa; each trip recorded on immigration records. She went third class. Eliza never married – had she done so, she would have been expected to leave her employment. Another relative, housekeeper to a ship's captain, married him in her fifties following his wife's death.

Socially situated between cleaning women and housekeeper were, in descending order, lady's maid, parlour maid, housemaid, kitchen maid, scullion. Mrs Beeton gives a Victorian view of the relationship between mistress and servant, explaining each servants' duties with gems like 'the lady's maid's day commences by seeing that their employer's dressing room is in order; that the housemaid had swept and dusted properly; that the fire is lighted and burns cheerfully' (chapter 68, 1909). A parlour maid in a small establishment replaced the footman and her tasks were: opening doors, bringing up and clearing away light meals, making beds, arranging flowers, 'all the lighter and less menial work of a housemaid, combining with these many little tasks that a mistress who kept only two servants would in all probability do for herself'.

In the morning, the parlour maid (conducting housemaid duties) wore 'a print gown and simple white cap'. She needn't wear the 'rough apron' of the housemaid. In the afternoon, a parlour maid's attire was a simply made black dress 'relieved by white collar, cuffs and cap and a pretty lace trimmed bib apron'. The lowly housemaid worked extremely long and hard hours; her duties in Mrs Beeton covered seven pages, the parlour maid's two.

In her 1863 *Guide to the Unprotected* (Chapter 1) Emma Galton explains how servants were paid and monitored. She recommended paying quarterly (Lady Day, Michaelmas, etc.) and, should a servant start mid-quarter and an employer's arithmetic be shaky (they were mere women), she directed her towards the Ready Reckoner. To prevent potential disputes, she advised servants countersign a stamped receipt. Galton pointed out they could be paid monthly should they wish and 'in the event of bankruptcy they are entitled to be paid a sum not exceeding three months' wages in full and have the preference of other creditors'.

Many employers supplied uniforms whereas others expected staff to provide their own clothing. Some had additional perks, with

Emma Galton advocating, 'At the time of hiring, in order to avoid further disputes, it is necessary to come to a distinct understanding whether the Employer or Servant provide washing, and whether tea, sugar and beer, are or are not included in the wages.'

In a concise 1857 guide, *The Rights, Duties, and Relations of Domestic Servants, their Masters and Mistresses*, *https://archive. org/stream/rightsdutiesand01baylgoog#page/n6/mode/2up barrister*, T Henry Bailiss explained the legal (and male) perspective of avoiding unpleasant staff disputes. He covered: hiring and firing; wages; writing *character* (references in modern parlance) and actions to take if they were false; livery; accidents; embezzlement; liability and how both servants and employers should treat each other. The appendix covered training institutions, servants' charitable institutions, financial information, plus exhortations for the family to say prayers with their servants.

Official Victorian employment law is surprisingly progressive considering how poorly it's perceived today. Bailiss reiterated servants were hired by the year, payable quarterly. After a month, either party can give a month's notice in writing. If an employer dismisses a servant, they must pay a month's salary without compensation for loss of food or clothing. A servant under the age of 16 hired from a workhouse or other institution must be visited twice a year by a representative confirming they're fed properly and not abused. As today, a servant was instantly dismissed for gross misconduct and theft, although Bailiss recommended that, rather than refuse a character reference, the facts should be presented. Clothing supplied to a servant was the property of the employer. If a servant was ill, the employer wasn't legally bound to pay doctor's fees even if the mistress had called one in. Although such bills could be paid by the parish, Bailiss hinted the employer was morally bound to cover them. Servants had no rights if they had an accident at work but if they damaged something could be sued for negligence. In reality, the cost was deducted from their wages.

A prospective employee faced imprisonment with hard labour if caught falsifying references as befell Eliza Wright, aged 23, convicted at Stockport Police Court in December 1909. She received a custodial sentence of nine months' hard labour – three months running concurrently for each false reference. Described as having an 'imperfect' education and no trade, it's understandable why she faked them. Her records plus photo can be seen by prior appointment in Criminals Album 1, Manchester Police Museum (Chapter 3). In 1911, she was an inmate at all-women's St Faith's Rescue Home for 'fallen and friendless girls', Leeds, a waitress, married two years but childless.

With few reasonable options available, life was difficult for a dismissed female servant. If unable to find a job even in a less salubrious establishment, she might turn to prostitution.

Homes comparable to industrial schools (later incorporated into them, Chapter 2) rehabilitated dismissed female servants before they resorted to prostitution; some are listed in Henry T Bailiss' book. One such under the charge of two matrons was the Tre-Wint, Hackney, which could accommodate up to twenty women. When Bailiss published his book, it housed fourteen over the age of 16, with laundry room, drying grounds and mangling room. Girls stayed a minimum of a year at a cost of 3s 6d covered by income from the laundry and benefactors. In 1881 it was Trewint Industrial Home, 201 Mare Street (RG11 311/14/20) three doors from the Elizabeth Fry Refuge (Chapter 3). The girls, ranging in age from 14 to 16, were enumerated as 'scholars' and their matron was Catherine Stowell aged just 26. For more about such homes see *www.childrens homes. org.uk.*

The Female Servants' Home Society, established 1836, supplied temporary housing for out of work London servants at two centres, 21 Nutford Place (women paid 1s 6d a week rent) and 110 Hatton Gardens (1s a week). Lodging in Nutford Place, 1851 (HO 107/1489/551/12), were thirty-six female house servants aged 16 to 64, hailing from as far as Antigua (West Indies), South Wales and Scotland. All were unmarried although three were widows. There was a residence for ageing servants at Raven Row, Mile End, from at least the mid-1850s where women received an annual pension of £10 paid for by donations, subscriptions and patrons.

In order to support girls relocating from the countryside for jobs in an urban area, the Girls' Friendly Society (GFS) *https://girls friendlysociety.org.uk* was founded in 1875 by several prominent members of the church: Reverend Thomas Vincent Fosbery, clergyman's daughter Mary Elizabeth Townsend (1841–1918), Archbishop of Canterbury's wife Catharine Tait (1819–78), Bishop of Winchester's wife Elizabeth Browne and Jane Senior (née Hughes 1828–77). This organisation was run by women for women, and the only male input was the treasurer's. The GFS, still in existence, offered cheap, safe lodgings for girls taking up jobs in domestic service or factories. Its records are held at the Women's Library at the LSE; see Discovery.

There are various archives for servants although, for those working in ordinary families, you're unlikely to find anything other than revealed in the census. Surviving records for large estates may include diaries and wage books held at the estate itself or in CROs. Harewood House, Yorkshire, *http://servants.harewood.org* has digitised over 1,000 servants' records from 1790. Housemaid Lucy Bonsell earned £12 a year in 1874. In 1892, kitchen maid Mary Fairbrass received £14 per annum. Compare this with footman John Douglas earning more than twice as much, £30, the same year. The site explains various roles within the estate, e.g. maid, kitchen and house maid. Chatsworth's archives (1700–1950) *www.chatsworth.org* are onsite and, at the time of writing, researched by PhD students. For ancestors working at Longleat, the archives have been digitised but access is undertaken by estate library staff for a fee. See *www.longleat.co.uk/about/library-and-archives*. Longleat is not alone in charging fees.

TNA Discovery will help locate them. Some family history societies hold information for large estates but prepare for disappointment. I've seen many online posts but few helpful replies although you might strike lucky.

Bibliography and Further Reading

Adams, Samuel and Sarah, *The Complete Servant; being a Practical Guide to the Peculiar Duties and Business of All Descriptions of Servants*, Knight & Lacey, 1825 *https://archive.org/stream/b21530786#page/n3/mode/2up*

Bailiss, T Henry, *On the Rights, Duties, and Relations of Domestic Servants and their Masters and Mistresses*, Sampson, Low & Son, 1857, *https://archive.org/details/rightsdutiesand01baylgoog*

Beeton, Isabella, *Mrs Beeton's Book of Household Management*, first published 1861

Higgs, Michelle, *Servants' Stories: Life Below Stairs in their Own Words 1800–1950, Pen & Sword, 2015*

Lethbridge, Lucy, *Servants: A Downstairs View of Twentieth-Century Britain,* Bloomsbury, 2013

May, Trevor, *The Victorian Servant,* Bloomsbury Shire, 1998

Sambrook, Pamela, *Keeping their Place: Domestic Service in the Country House,* History Press, 2005

BEERHOUSE KEEPERS, PUBLICANS AND LICENSED VICTUALLERS

Although the majority of licensees were men, my family is full of female licensed victuallers and beerhouse keepers. Many took over a licence on widowhood but must have worked in the business on a day-to-day basis before the husband's death although not always recorded on the census.

One woman, referred to in my family as Aunt Louie, was Louisa Ann Martin. Family legend insists she made so much money running public houses that she retired to upmarket Lytham St Anne's. After her death, her substantial estate of £13,334 (1924) was divvied up and her surviving relatives each bought a house.

Her secret to success? A former teacher, Aunt Louie married into the pub trade. Mother-in-law and widow Elizabeth Martin was licensed victualler at The Clock Face, Toad Lane, Rochdale (birthplace of the Co-operative movement) until the family upped sticks for Poulton le Fylde.

Louisa Ann Martin (1860–1924) licensee publican extraordinaire. Author's collection © Adèle Emm

The Golden Ball, Poulton le Fylde, Lancashire, run by Louisa Ann Martin between 1896 and 1901. Author's collection © Adèle Emm

Anecdotal evidence claimed that, when Louie took over a pub, she installed pianists and entertainers, billiards and card rooms to improve takings – clearly seen in the c1904 photograph of the Golden Ball Hotel, Poulton le Fylde. Unafraid of embracing technology, the Golden Ball's phone number in 1898 was 4.

Licensing laws have existed since 1552 but for the timescale covered by this book, legislation was:

- 1828: All alehouses, inns and victualling houses required justice's licences and excise licences. The government wanted to decrease the amount of hard liquor (gin) drunk by working people.
- 1830 Beerhouse Act permitted houses of a certain value to sell beer with an excise licence (2 guineas); beerhouses proliferated. Open up to eighteen hours a day from 4 a.m. until 10 p.m., a beershop sold ale to be drunk off premises (off-licence) whereas

in a beerhouse, ale was drunk on the premises. Within six years, there were 46,000 beershops and beerhouses in the country.

- 1840 Beerhouse Act ensured people running beerhouses possessed the deeds and lived there. Designed to control civil disorder (drunkenness). Effectively, if a female ancestor was a beerhouse keeper in the 1841 census, she lived on site.
- 1869 Wine and Beerhouse Act required a justice's certificate to obtain an excise licence. More control on both beerhouses and public houses.
- 1872 Intoxicating Liquor (licensing) Act restricted opening hours for public houses and beerhouses. In towns, pubs closed at midnight, 11 p.m. in the country. Adulterating beer with salt to make a drinker thirstier was banned. Licences from justices required for retailers selling beer and wine.

Managing a beerhouse or pub entailed extensive hours as any woman married to a publican, beerhouse keeper or licensee in her own right would testify. Subject to scrutiny from justices and police, running a 'disorderly house' threatened her licence – often reported in local newspapers.

Simon Fowler explains the working life of barmaid and waitress in *www.sfowler.force9.co.uk/page_24.htm.* Seventy hours rising to a hundred a week was not unusual, but the norm was a ten-plus-hour day with perhaps Sunday off. The longest shifts were generally for those working in public houses – she usually lived in – and railway refreshment bars. However, because of train timetables, stations had staggered shifts; one girl started at 7 a.m. working until 9.30 p.m. and a colleague began 11.30 a.m., finishing at 11 p.m. Theatre barmaids had shorter shifts, starting just before matinees and leaving after an evening performance, mornings were free. Barmaids were paid around 10s a week plus tips which must have compensated for those long hours.

Contemporary newspapers are excellent sources for background information although mainly for negative reasons; a victualler/publican taken to the magistrate for infringements of licensing laws or brawls on their premises. In August 1867, Ann Ryan, drowning her sorrows having been dismissed from Rochdale's The Clock Face (before the Martins ran it), was fined 5s and costs or seven days' imprisonment for being drunk and incapable.

Trade directories, although useful, largely just confirm dates, addresses and licensees – although one revealed the Golden Ball's phone number.

Surviving Brewster Sessions records (annual meeting of licensing justices for granting, renewal and transfer of licences to sell intoxicating liquor) are held locally, as are Quarter Sessions archives; see TNA. The word *brewster* originally referred to a woman who brewed beer.

Beerhouse keeper Elizabeth Harris (1829–1900) ran the 'Pig and Whistle', Newport Pagnell. Author's collection © Adèle Emm

As pubs and beerhouses are so ingrained in the British psyche, specialist websites feature pubs with photographs of long demolished buildings. Some local libraries have folders and archives on individual hostelries; try there and follow up with the CRO.

Aficionados publish pub directories of their local area, e.g. *Sheffield Pubs, Landlords and Landladies* by Peter Tuffrey (Fonthill, 2012); Newport Pagnell's *One More for the Road* by Donald Hurst and Dennis Mynard (Newport Pagnell Historic Society, 1999); or Rob Magee's *A Directory of Ashton Pubs and their Licensees.* There are others and many name licensees, dates and anecdotes. A list of books about the history of the public house and localised pub histories is found at *www.genguide.co.uk/source/publican-brewery-and-licensed-victuallers-records-occupations/127*.

The Licensed Victuallers Asylum, formed 1826, ran almshouses for former publicans and those who had worked in the industry (Chapter 4). Records for the Old Kent Road asylum, Camberwell (from 1842), are held at the Guildhall.

149

The London Metropolitan Archives information sheet No. 45 for Licensed Victuallers Records Leaflet is at *www.cityoflondon.gov.uk /things-to-do/london-metropolitan-archives/visitor-information/Documents /45-licensed-victuallers-records.pdf* and lists what records survive, for what years and where they are held.

The Pub History website at *https://pubshistory.com* features pubs around the country and often names historical licensees (e.g. Berkshire, Essex, Kent, Surrey, Cumberland, Lancashire, Yorkshire) plus information on the Victuallers Asylum. Also *www.midlands pubs.co.uk/glossary/beer-houses.htm.* The Closed Pubs website *www.closedpubs.co.uk* is less useful.

Although not pubs, I must include Nippies (waitresses) working for the ubiquitous Lyons teashops (from 1894), or Corner Houses (from 1909). These respectable places were where women felt comfortable meeting friends. Peter Bird's volunteer website *www.kzwp.com/lyons/index.htmj* shares hundreds of photographs and biographical information for staff not just in teashops but elsewhere in the company, e.g. bakeries.

Bibliography and Further Reading

Barclay, William, *Handy-Book for Licensed Victuallers, Brewers, Wine Retailers, Beer and Refreshment House Keepers, and Post Masters, Including The Public House Closing Act, 1864, with Instructions for Beginners and an Appendix of Useful Forms,* Routledge, Warne& Routledge, 1865 at *https://archive.org/details/handybookforlic 00barcgoog*

Fowler, Simon, *Researching Brewery and Publican Ancestors,* Family History Partnership, 2009: his link to further research is *www.sfowler.force9.co.uk/page_12.htm*

Gibson, J and Hunter, J, *Victuallers' Licences: Records for Family and Local Historians,* Federation of Family History Societies, 1994

COTTAGE INDUSTRIES – E.G. LACE MAKING, STRAW BONNET MAKING

Cottage industries employing women working from home were

largely regionally based; lace was produced in Buckinghamshire, Bedfordshire, Northamptonshire, Devon and Nottingham, although, as Nottinghamshire lace was machine-produced, most workers here were male. Straw plaiting for bonnets was based around Luton, Buckinghamshire and Bedfordshire. Other similar cottage industries such as basket weaving, button and glove making were largely where agricultural labourer's wives and children could supplement the family coffers.

Working conditions were difficult in damp, dark, poky homes and, in order to fulfil agent set quotas, hours could be punishing. Agents, nearly always men, supplied raw materials (occasionally charging for them), and a family buckled down risking a heavy fine or penalty if they failed to manufacture the specified amount. Children as young as 5 or 6 helped out with this piece work.

For lace making history and genealogical research, the Cooper Newton Museum, Olney, Buckinghamshire *www.cowperand newtonmuseum.org.uk* provides a good background. Some family history societies and communities have compiled articles of local industry workers, for instance, Stoke Goldington Association at *http:// www.mkheritage.co.uk/sga/index.html.*

Local CROs are the best resource for cottage industries but individual genealogical information may be sparse or non-existent. Newspapers reported events like Pillow Lace Association meetings (i.e. *Buckingham Advertiser and Free Press*, 27 June 1891) where several Ladies (including Lady Spencer, Mrs Creighton, wife of the Bishop of Peterborough) promoted improvements to the industry.

DRESSMAKERS/SEAMSTRESSES/MILLINERS

Women trained through an apprenticeship to become dressmaker, seamstress and milliner. Seamstresses repaired clothing or specialised in making blouses or skirts. A milliner made hats. However, many diversified. A dressmaker/milliner in a census produced the whole package.

Because they ran their own business and had a skill, it was more respectable than factory work but hours could be more punishing

Seamstress shop (including my grand aunt) c1904. Notice the Singer sewing machine in the centre. Several girls hold scissors, another pair attached to clothing (top row left). Author's collection © Adèle Emm

under worse conditions; women working at home supplied their own light and heating or did without. Agents provided cloth but not needles, thimble, thread or trimmings. Some agents supplied slop shops; 'slops' were cheap, ready-made clothing produced under sweated labour and we have already seen how Lucretia Jefferies died of starvation working for one (Chapter 1). Thomas Hood's poem 'Song of the Shirt' published anonymously in *Punch*, 1843, exposed a seamstress' gruelling life.

Life was also hard for women slaving in couturiers' backrooms. Apprentices aged 12 worked overnight without pay because they were being trained.

Following the introduction of the sewing machine in the late 1850s, few women could afford to buy one outright so paid for it on the never-never or rented it from their agent. The sewing machine is credited as one of the most important inventions ever. It drastically reduced the time required to produce clothes. By hand, a woman sewed thirty-five stitches a minute; a machine stitched 3,000. A dress shirt with intricate stitching took fourteen hours by hand; one hour fifteen minutes by machine. A dress taking ten hours by hand was run-up in one.

At first, the price of clothing dropped dramatically and even mill workers could afford more than work clothes and Sunday best. But because twenty sewing machines did the work of sixty women, wages were suppressed and dressmakers and seamstresses lost their jobs. By the 1860s, factories employed rows of women working long hours at their sewing machines.

The 1867 Factory Act restricted working hours for women and young people to twelve a day for any factory employing more than fifty people – so clothing factories employed forty-nine women instead. Anyone desperate to keep her job took work home to finish. By the Edwardian era, for sewing a dozen blouses selling for 18s to £1 each, a seamstress might earn 10s a week.

Self-employed women in suburbs, towns and villages advertised their services in newspapers and directories, revealing inter-census addresses. In 9 May 1874 edition of *Buckinghamshire Advertiser and Free Press*, Mrs Webb of Market Hill, Buckingham, promoted her summer collection of millinery, mantles (short outdoor cloaks) and costumes plus securing an apprentice at the same time. The 1871 census (RG10/1423/22/35) reveals widow, Rebecca Webb (born c1831), running a successful business employing daughter Catherine, several milliners, dressmakers and servants. For anyone descended from her, the advert refines her expertise. In Kelly's 1883 Buckinghamshire directory, Mrs Rebecca Webb has relocated to West Street, still trading as milliner dressmaker.

Dressmakers commonly specialised. Miss Russell, milliner, dress and mantle maker of 2 Beaufort Place, St Thomas, Exeter, advertised in the *Western Times*, July 1876, as formerly working in London's West End. She now supplied paper patterns plus 'Wedding and Mourning Orders promptly executed'.

Surviving apprentice records are generally held in CROs and not always indexed.

THE LAND

At the beginning of the nineteenth century, most people lived in the countryside but, as the industrial revolution, agricultural slumps and economic crises bit, migrated towards towns and cities for employment. In the 1861 census, as Josephine Butler informed both her supporters and detractors, '43,964 women are returned as outdoor agricultural labourers – a fact worthy of remembrance when it is said that women are too weak to serve in haberdashers' shops'.

Working alongside their menfolk, women undertook the slightly less physical tasks; picking stones, weeding corn, gleaning, threshing, sowing, or working in brew-house, dairy or buttery as well as supplementary cottage industry work. Should her husband die, she might take on his job. Is this why Dennes Gibbs (née Skull, born Wiltshire 1832) was enumerated in 1871 (RG10/1910/25/20) as shepherd? By 1901, she was a domestic nurse. The same applied to farmers' wives; Yorkshire born Harriet Kingston (née Bennison, 1845–1911) was a widowed farmer of 276 acres in Flamborough, 1881.

Any female farm servant in a census was usually married to an 'ag lab' taken on with husband and children at hirings; she helped in the farmhouse. Such hiring fairs, depending on region, took place after harvest around Michaelmas (29 September). A contract, sealed with shake of hand and small coin, generally lasted a year. A family, therefore, worked anywhere within walking distance i.e. 30 mile radius of a market town, explaining why they migrated from village to village near their recorded place of birth.

Women ag labs arrived at work two hours later than her husband having prepared breakfast and lunch beforehand (traditional ploughman's lunch was bread and cheese), and finished work early to prepare the family's evening meal. Like men, she worked a six-day week, Sunday being Sabbath and church.

Harvest was crucial for everyone's survival. An entire family mucked in at the fields; two or three women plus children followed the reaper tying harvested cereal into sheaves. In fruit-growing areas, women picked the fruit.

Women generally wore a ubiquitous working apron protecting dress, plus bonnet. When gleaning (gathering post-harvest leftover grain), women wore a 'gladrag', an apron with large pockets at the front where gleanings (the grain) were collected. Traditionally, gleanings were an entitlement for country folk and augmented their income.

In 1870, female farmers were denied membership of the Royal Agricultural Society (RAS) providing access to advantageous terms for feeding stuffs and soil examinations. By 1882, home-educated spinster Eleanor Anne Ormerod (1828–1901) had been admitted. This extraordinary woman became, amongst other accolades, adviser to the Board of Agriculture 1885–90 and the first Lady Fellow of the Meteorological Society (1878). The RAS archives, copies of her books and correspondence are at the Museum of English Rural Life (MERL), Reading University *www.reading.ac.uk/merl*; for the RAS holding see *www.reading.ac.uk/merl/collections/archives_a_to_z/merl-sr_rase.aspx*. MERL has a run of the *Journal of the Royal Agricultural Society of England* (1840–2000) on open shelves. The museum offers an insight into our agricultural ancestors' daily lives.

Surviving resources for land workers are held locally but, due to their low status and large-scale illiteracy, there may be little to find. Usual suspects are farm diaries for larger estates where they may be listed in wage books although, because women were part of a family package, they're often invisible. Check bastardy examinations, workhouse, resettlement and court records, etc. but you may pursue a long journey to reveal nothing.

Bibliography and Further Reading

Brown, Jonathan, *Tracing Your Rural Ancestors*, Pen & Sword, 2011
Eveleigh, David J, *The Victorian Farmer*, Shire, 1991
Goddard, Nicholas, *Harvests of Change: History of the Royal Agricultural Society of England, 1838–1988*, Quiller, 1988
Handford, Kay, *The Agricultural Labourer in 19th Century England*, Grosvenor House, 2011

Kebbel, T E, *The Agricultural Labourer, a Short Summary of his Position*, W. H. Allen, 1887 (earlier edn 1870)

Mingay, Gordon E, *Rural Life in Victorian England, 1800–1900*, Sutton, 1990

Thompson, Flora, *Lark Rise to Candleford*, OUP, 1945

Waller, Ian, *My Ancestor was an Agricultural Labourer*, Society of Genealogists, 2014

MILL AND FACTORY WORKERS

The biggest change in gender employment was the industrial revolution and introduction of large-scale manufacturing processes – factories and mills. Before this, the majority of silk, wool, linen and cotton weavers were men operating the hard, physical graft of a hand-loom in the family home.

Also working at home (hence the expression 'cottage industry') were female spinners, six of whom beavered away to supply enough yarn for one weaver. A male clothier or manufacturer acted as agent for whom spinners, weavers, bleachers and dyers worked, a nineteenth-century production manager if you like, coordinating each component of which all, bar spinning, was undertaken by men.

By the 1830s, spinning, previously the province of a woman at home, had become the job of a man in a mill: in 1833, 60,000 men worked in cotton mills compared to 5,000 women. Behind engineers and managers, always men, male spinners earned the highest wages albeit as piece work remunerated by amount produced. However, towards the end of the nineteenth century, textile mill employees, even spinners, were predominantly female – and paid considerably less than their male counterparts.

In 1851, the textile industry was the third largest overall employer, but the second for women behind domestic service. In 1861, 131 women were employed in this industry for every 100 men: by 1881 it was 164 women to 100 men.

By the mid-1860s, many male hand-loom weavers had been declared bankrupt (announced in *The Gazette www.thegazette.co.uk* and/or local newspaper). Eventually, hundreds of women were employed in huge weaving sheds (by the early twentieth century, an experienced female weaver oversaw up to sixteen looms) with a handful of men overseeing them.

Although textile mills were countrywide, there were regional specialisms: North West England and New Lanark, Scotland, manufactured cotton products; jute and linen were based in Dundee; wool in Yorkshire. Outnumbering men by three to one, more than half the working population in Dundee, 1900, were women in jute mills.

In charge of each floor or operational area was a man, the overseer or overlooker, managing perhaps hundreds of women each paid less than any man employed there.

Working conditions in textile mills were onerous; twelve-hour shifts and unpaid lunch-breaks meant women commonly worked thirteen hour days in oily, noisy rooms where temperatures (to prevent cotton breaking) were over 90°F (32°C). It was common to eat lunch at the factory, heated up on the boilers. Women quickly learned to lip read, many stone deaf within a year.

Fines were common for insubordination, lateness (factory doors shut, latecomers locked out), not picking up cotton (a fire hazard). Some wore clogs but most preferred working in bare feet to pick up cotton strands between their toes.

Health and safety was rudimentary; although hair was tied back, long skirts and aprons caught in machinery resulting in horrific injuries. Most industrial accidents (newspapers provide the best contemporary resource) took place towards the end of the working day when women lost concentration or fell asleep through exhaustion.

With no sickness pay, welfare or National Health Service, an accident or illness was devastating for family finances and factories often had a whip round to help an injured employee. In January 1830, a girl called Dixon (no first name reported) working in a flax mill owned by Fell, Son and Pearson at Ellers, Ulverston, became entangled with machinery causing injuries so grave her hand was amputated. The employers organised the 'humane act' of a subscription to provide for her future.

Fires, regularly reported in newspapers, were common in hot factories where combustible fibres hung in the hot air and wooden floorboards were greasy with oil. Flames rapidly spread following a spark from a machine, clog-iron or boiler explosion. Even if nobody lost their life, the destruction of a mill meant nowhere to work and consequently no income.

When fire destroyed James Livesey's cotton mill four miles from Blackburn, Lancashire, 19 March 1846, there was £10,000–£15,000 damage to a building insured for £7,000. The *Manchester Courier and Lancashire General Advertiser*, 21 March 1846, reported six women on an upper floor escaping by the skin of their teeth down ropes wound around their waists, the last stretch via a ladder.

> It was most distressing to see the confusion and alarm of the hands who reside close to the mill . . . men, women and children were to be seen carrying out their furniture, and throwing it into the fields at some distance from the mill. Fortunately, these buildings were saved . . . It is to be regretted that several hundreds of workpeople will be for some time thrown out of employment.

Many mill records have not survived – an important exception being Quarry Bank (Chapter 2). Those that do are usually in CROs. Information is variable, financial records or floor plans common but often little personnel data. Also try newspapers.

As people lived near their workplace, comparing census address to a map reveals the nearest mill. To discourage workers trained in one mill flitting to a nearby one for higher wages, neighbouring mill owners offered the same rate so, if a worker changed jobs, they moved rather than commute a few more yards.

An interesting online cotton industry project produced by Manchester Libraries is *www.spinningtheweb.org.uk* with sections on history, machinery, technological progress and employment.

The Cotton Famine

Even though it was 4,000 miles from Lancashire and north Cheshire, the American Civil War (1861–5) had a catastrophic effect on the region. By blockading Confederate ports, the Union Army prevented the export of raw cotton. With no cotton, mills went on short time or closed. The workforce was locked out and, with no welfare state, people sold what they had to feed themselves and their children. Families moved to progressively cheaper accommodation.

Relief Committees were established to dispense welfare and organise enterprises offering a source of income for those affected. Edwin Waugh's (1817–90) *Home-life of the Lancashire Factory Folk during the Cotton Famine* (online at *www.gutenberg.org/files/10126/ 10126.txt*) published heartrending songs and poems, often in Lancashire dialect, to raise funds.

Several towns including Bury ran sewing schools and registers (not indexed at the time of writing) give women's names, addresses, attendance dates and earnings. The schools were run by educated middle-class woman, also often named. Surviving records, minutes and other documents are in CROs see TNA.

Norman Longmate's comprehensive 1978 book, *The Hungry Mills: The Story of the Lancashire Cotton Famine, 1862–1865*, is excellent for background and social repercussions. A plethora of books and written material on the textile industry is in bookshops, libraries and on the internet.

NURSE AND MIDWIFE

Under the pens of Charlotte Brontë and Charles Dickens, Sarah Gamp (*Martin Chuzzlewit*, 1844) and Grace Poole (*Jane Eyre*, 1847) were grotesque inebriates – this was how nursing was perceived. In reality, it was a dreadful job performed by widows, single mothers and dismissed servants; in social hierarchy, regarded only as slightly superior to prostitution.

Nurses worked sixteen- to seventeen-hour shifts, seven days a week, fifty-two weeks a year. Pre-Florence Nightingale (1820–1910), they cleaned wards at a time when alcohol was prescribed for health reasons (how time has changed) and where patients were frequently drunk and unruly. Many were paupers from the workhouse aged 60 to 80 set to work for 1d a week (yes, one penny), maximum 1s a month plus beer. In 1819, the word *menial* was interchangeable with 'nurse'. In some early nineteenth-century hospitals, assistant nurses supported surgeons removing soiled bandages, giving enemas and emetics, fed patients and delivered beer. By the middle of the century, John Flint South, Senior Surgeon at St Thomas' Hospital, believed women nurses and nursing assistants should be called 'ward servants'.

In a census, nursing was recorded a number of ways; not all were the lowest of the low:

- servant/nurse/children's nurse
- matron
- ward attendant
- monthly nurse (like Mrs Gamp). There were more than 3,000 in 1881. A monthly nurse (or midwife) was present at a mother's lying-in and for a month following childbirth. Doubling as women who laid out the dead, childbirth was so dangerous, she might birth baby then lay out both mother and new-born.
- sick nurse; night nurse; day nurse
- night watcher, which could be a night watchman, an entirely different job – the address is the clue. At St Thomas' Hospital, London, night watchers worked fifteen hour shifts from 7 p.m. in winter, 8 p.m. summer cleaning wards and watching patients for a change in condition when they informed the sister. The least trained of all nursing staff.
- SMS; Subordinate or Subsidiary Medical Services
- 'poor law official' could signify a nurse in a Poor Law hospital

Elizabeth Fry's Nursing Institution (1840) offered on-the-job training for up to 100 women from respectable working-class backgrounds and predates Nightingale's School. Some Catholic convents provided nurses.

Edith Cavell (1865–1915) memorial, St Martin's Place, London. Trained at Royal London Hospital, Whitechapel, 1896–8. Matron at Belgium's first nursing school. Shot for treason by the Germans in the First World War. © Adèle Emm

But the biggest influence on the profession was Florence Nightingale, singlehandedly responsible for revolutionising the status of nurse from menial to highly regarded profession. Much has been written about this formidable woman who, following her experience at the Crimean War, raised £55,000 in 1855 to establish the Nightingale Fund. The first professional School of Nursing opened 24 June 1860 at St Thomas' Hospital, London, ironically where surgeon John Flint South had made his disparaging remarks.

Twenty to thirty female trainees per class lived in private on-site rooms with a common room. Their first year was spent in the Home. They trained on the ward during the second and third, plus attended lectures delivered by medical superintendents, doctors and surgeons. Sick trainees were nursed in their own hospital. Many were from illiterate working-class backgrounds so, on completion, women received a small bursary and placement in an institution or hospital under a middle-class matron.

In one fell stroke, Nightingale raised hospitals from filthy places where people went to die to clean, professional institutions run by efficient caring women. Twenty years later, former students were matrons managing hospitals worldwide.

Amongst them was Lydia Constable. Born 1840 in Aldenham, Hertfordshire, fourth child of an agricultural labourer, she was solidly working class. In 1861 and 1871, she was in service to the family of Henry Burrows, Perpetual Curate of Christchurch St Pancras, first as housemaid then nurse. At some point, she trained under the Nightingale Fund at St Thomas' and in 1881, was infirmary nurse at Kensington and Chelsea District School.

Named in homage to General Gordon (1830–85) killed at Khartoum, Gordon Boys' Home, Woking, opened in 1888, with Lydia Constable its first matron. A press report describes her demesne as 'the cosy hospital under the matronly charge of its cheery Nightingale norm'. Now a coeducational boarding school, Gordon's early history is at *www.childrenshomes.org.uk/Woking Gordon.*

162

Miss Lydia Constable, matron of Gordon Boys' Home from 1888 to 1897. Author's collection © Adèle Emm

Lydia was summarily sacked for 'being absent without leave' August 1897, with notice to leave by 18 October. Nightingale interceded. She wrote to Chairman Sir George Higginson (28 August 1897), pleading Sister Constable's absence was 'based on a misunderstanding' and 'insufficient grounds for dismissal' for 'a strictly trustworthy and truthful woman and an excellent nurse' who having worked there for over nine years should receive severance pay (*compensation* in Nightingale's words). An amazing testimonial, the letter is online at University of Kansas Medical Centre website.

Sir Henry Burdett's book, *How to Become a Nurse, the Nursing Profession* (*archive.org/details/b29012995*; pre-1901, with later editions) explains nursing in its variety of guises; Poor Law hospitals, mental nursing, army and navy nursing, midwifery, private and children's nursing and cottage hospitals. It lists all institutions plus conditions under which nurses trained and worked.

To be taken on as a probationer in 1906, most institutions required women to be between 20 and 30 and prove a satisfactory 'character, education, health and physique'. Macclesfield General Infirmary, with sixty-six beds, had one matron, four sisters and nine probationers trained over three years. Benefits included two hours' recreation a day, two weeks' holiday a year and, although no salary for the initial year, women earned £15 in their second and £18 in the last. A sister's first year remuneration was £25, uniform and laundry provided.

To obtain a job at Belfast's Society of Providing Nurses for the Sick Poor, she must have fulfilled three years' training at an official institution, and earned £45 per annum with three weeks' holiday, indoor and outdoor uniform, local board and lodging.

Nursing became an attractive proposition for ambitious, working-class girls like Lydia Constable, bestowing a status hard to achieve anywhere else, a stipend and place to live whilst training plus lifelong skill once qualified. These single women were never a burden on their family.

By the early 1900s, there were plenty of nurse training centres including workhouses. Manchester Workhouse, Crumpsall, 1911 (RG14/467/34-39/24204), employed many a single woman as matron, assistant matron, night superintendent, charge nurse, probationer and hospital attendant. 'Lunatic attendants' were listed under servant. A photograph of the workhouse in 1906 plus further information can be found on *www.workhouses.org.uk/Manchester.* Its surviving workhouse records are at Manchester CRO (Ref GB127.M326), see the website *www.manchester.gov.uk/directory_ record/212444/crumpsall_workhouse/category/1371/workhouse.*

What happened to Miss Constable after losing her job at Woking Boys' Home? Four years later, she has a more lowly position, 'sick nurse' on 'own account' living with her widowed sister in St Albans. By 1911, she's a 'trained nurse' alone in two rooms in the Edwardian version of sheltered housing, Marlborough Buildings, St Albans (Chapter 4). As residents conformed to strict criteria to be admitted, she must have reclaimed her reputation.

The concept of *district nursing* was founded in Liverpool in the late 1860s by philanthropist William Rathbone (1819–1902). Having originally employed a Mary Robinson in 1859 to nurse his dying wife, he later persuaded her to nurse some of Liverpool's poorest in their homes. Because of its proximity to Ireland, Liverpool had been inundated from the 1840s by impoverished Irish fleeing the famine, many subsisting in deplorable conditions. So appalled was Mary Robinson by what she witnessed, it became her vocation. Following Florence Nightingale's example and advice, William Rathbone set up a home and training school attached to Liverpool Infirmary, completed in 1863. For the Queen's Nursing Institute heritage page about district nursing, see *http://qniheritage.org.uk.*

Midwifery was initially another low-status job conducted by women with some experience (anecdotal evidence mentions prostitutes charging for her midwifery services in gin). The Midwives Institute (founded c1880) improved education and professionalism and was instrumental in passing the 1902 Midwives Act. This ensured training, qualification and certification, with a £5 magistrate's fine for any woman practising without sufficient documentation. By 1910, only certified midwives could attend childbirth. Their monthly journal, *Nursing Notes and Midwives Chronicles* (from 1887), lists holders of a midwifery diploma issued by obstetrical societies. Records are at the Royal College of Midwives at the Royal College of Obstetricians and Gynaecologists. The information sheet for family historians is at *www.rcog.org.uk/en/*

guidelines-research-services/library-services/archives-and-heritage/ resources -for-family-historians-at-the-rcog. The Central Midwives Board Roll of Midwives for England and Wales, 1902–83, is at TNA, reference DV7. Libraries such as London's Wellcome Library *https://wellcome library.org* hold copies.

The Midwives Roll 1904–59 (courtesy Wellcome Foundation) is on Ancestry. For midwives practising before the register, you may find them in court records or newspapers, especially if tried for attempting to procure an abortion. The case of London midwife Annie Vale, 39, was reported in *Dublin Medical Press*, 20 November 1861, for attempting to procure an abortion for Mrs Anne Horne on 6 October. Tried at the Old Bailey, she was acquitted. If convicted under the 1861 Offences Against the Person Act, she would have received life imprisonment. Annie, a woman with easy access to drugs, lived with her husband, Benjamin Vale, surgeon licentiate of Apothecary Hall, at 6 Henry Street, Limehouse (RG9/286/93/11). He, too, had a brush with the Old Bailey (*www.oldbaileyonline.org/ images.jsp?doc=186111250051*).

Compare her conviction with that of midwife Elizabeth Goddard, 45, condemned to death six months earlier at Leicester assizes for the murder by surgical operation of Sarah Kellam (*Dublin Medical Press*, 27 March 1861). Commuted to penal servitude, a few days following her conviction the 1861 census records a married prisoner in Leicester jail under initials EG, 45, midwife. In 1871, Elizabeth is home with Thomas, no occupation given for her.

The records of the Royal College of Nursing (RCN) have been digitised; their search form and family history guides are at *www.rcn.org.uk/library/services/family-history.* At the time of writing, RCN research is not free although RCN members are entitled to fifteen minutes of free time. The general public pays £20 an hour for researching up to four names, however, if your nurse ancestor did not belong to any official nursing body, this service is not for you – the College will have no record of your ancestor. Their research takes up to ten days after completing a form with as much information as possible including training dates and institutions if known. Results are returned via email. Under Data Protection Acts, the RCN cannot provide details of nurses who may still be alive. Information held by the RCN includes:

- name
- membership number
- address
- place of work
- place of training

The London Metropolitan Archives information leaflet No. 36, *History of Nursing; Major Sources at London Metropolitan Archives* is online. The LMA holds records for:

- Training Institution for Nurses for Hospitals, families and sick poor at St John's House (1848). The reference number for the LMA is HO1/ST/SJ and these nurses worked at King's College Hospital in 1856 and Charing Cross Hospital between 1866 and 1883
- London Biblewomen and Nurses Mission (Ranyard Mission and Ranyard Nurses) 1868; Ref A/RY
- Metropolitan and National Association for Providing Nurses for the Sick Poor (1875). Supported by Florence Nightingale, this association trained and provided nursing staff to visit the poor in their homes. Ref Ms14618–55, Ms 14811–12, Ms 14891–3

Around 250 historical nursing periodicals are held at the heritage centre of the RCN and *www.rcn.org.uk/library/collections/special-collections/historical-nursing-journals* although you must make an appointment to view them. Journals include: *The Nursing Record/ British Journal of Nursing* (1888–1956), *The Nursing Mirror* (1907–85) and *The Nursing Times* (1905–).

Some RCN records such as UK and Ireland Nursing Registers 1898–1968, and Queen's Nursing Institute and Roll of Nursing, 1891–1931 have been digitised and are available via Ancestry.

Burdett's Official Nursing Directory 1898, is also on Ancestry and may include date of birth, address, maiden name, date of appointment and where educated. Lydia Constable's reference reads, 'Gordon Boys' Home, Woking. Nurse Matron since August 1888. Pro., Nightingale Home, March 1878 to March 1879; staff nurse St Thomas Hospital to Sept 1880; Sister St Marylebone Inf., Nov 1881 to July 1888.'

Try newspapers at the BNA, FindMyPast or locally on microfilm etc.

Bibliography and Further Reading

Burdett, H C, *How to Become a Nurse: The Nursing Profession, How and Where to Train: Being a Guide for Trained Nurses in their Work and to Training for the Profession of a Nurse: with Particulars of Nurse Training Schools in the United Kingdom and Abroad and an Outline of the Principal Laws Affecting Nurses, etc.* London, 1908, *https://archive.org/details/b29012995*

Cohen, Susan, *The District Nurse*, Bloomsbury Shire, 2010

Cohen, Susan, *The Midwife*, Bloomsbury Shire, 2016

Helmstadter, Carol, and Godden, Judith, *Nursing before Nightingale, 1815–1899*, Ashgate, 2011

Higgs, Michelle, *Tracing Your Medical Ancestors*, Pen & Sword, 2011

Mitton, Lavinia, *The Victorian Hospital*, Bloomsbury Shire, 2001

Nightingale, Florence, *Notes on Nursing, What it is and What it is Not*, London, 1859, *https://archive.org/stream/notesnursing what00nigh#page/n7/mode/2up*; Florence Nightingale Museum, St Thomas' Hospital, London, *www.florence-nightingale. co.uk/?v=79cba1185463*. Her letters are being digitised see *http://hgar-srv3.bu.edu/web/florence-nightingale*

Towler, Jean, and Bramall, Joan, *Midwives in History*, Croom Helm, 1986

POST OFFICE AND TELEGRAPHISTS

The Post Office (PO), founded 1840, was one of the largest employers and amongst the earliest to take on women to work as sub-postmistresses and letter carriers; female clerks from 1870 and, from this year, any woman working as a telegraphist, became a PO employee. Effectively, as a branch of the civil service, prospective employees sat examinations in geography, mathematics, English and a foreign language – in 1876 Miss Buss (Chapter 2) boasted nine pupils passed that year. Flora Thompson's *Lark Rise to Candleford*, 1939, portrays a turn of the century post office headed by a female postmistress. Under PO regulations married woman were not employed, so, if she wed whilst in their service she must resign her post (rescinded 1946). The webpage *www.postalmuseum.org/discover/explore-online/postal-history/women* gives further details. The British Postal Service Appointment Books, 1737–1969, are on Ancestry and the Post Office archive is free to visit in person *www.postalmuseum.org/discover/collections/archive-collection/family-history.* For a history of women in the civil service see *www.civil servant.org.uk/women-history.html.*

SHOP KEEPER AND SHOP ASSISTANTS

Until the mid-nineteenth century, shop assistants were generally male and, because shops are businesses, the proprietor was also male; wives and daughters occasionally assisting him. Widows might continue a business (she'd worked uncredited hours before his death) perhaps retaining his name on the shop-front for continuity.

It must have been embarrassing for female customers to subject body and sartorial taste to men when buying, for instance, underwear. It was the rise of the department store from the 1850s (originally, these too employed men) which, once shopping was a popular pursuit for woman, employed women to serve them. By the late 1850s, it was a reputable and respectable job for working-class girls with aspirations; she must be presentable, well spoken, polite, confident with customers of a higher social standing and educated enough to do complicated arithmetic in her head – no electronic calculators or fancy automatic tills in those days.

Women working in owner-run shops not only had to serve customers but also cleaned the premises (as today) and displayed goods (ditto). Shops individually sourced merchandise so, should the owner be away, the assistant conducted negotiations with travelling salesmen. Shop girls generally lived in and are numerated thus in a census.

Activist and publisher Emily Faithfull (1835–95) promoted department store work for working class girls in her *Choice of a Business for Girls* (1864); it paid relatively well, £20 to £50 a year with board and lodgings included. This was commensurate, if not better than, that earned by better educated governesses and, Faithfull advocated, offered a more pleasant lifestyle than charring, factory or farm work.

Industrial diseases associated with shop-work largely due to 'standing-evil' for many hours were indigestion, varicose veins, swollen feet, anaemia, headaches and fainting.

Shops and emporiums advertised themselves in local newspapers. Mrs J T Tucker & Sons, for instance (I found no evidence for either a Mr or Mrs Tucker), of 243/244 High Street, Exeter, advertised a Ladies Outfitting and Underclothing business on page 5 of *Western Times*, 14 July 1876. Targeting the higher end of the market, her shop specialised in trousseaux (from £25) and baby clothing (layettes from £15). In the 1881 census, the household consisted entirely of female shop assistants; silk mercers, milliners, mantle makers, dressmakers, assistants and apprentices largely local Devonshire-born although one milliner hailed from Dublin and a handful from London and further afield. All were unmarried bar two widows, including a servant aged 60 who presumably did the cleaning. Evidently, the owners didn't live 'above the shop'.

Census figures show the rise in retail employment. In 1871, there were 120,000 female shop workers; 140,000 in 1881 and 250,000 by 1901. Although it's difficult to trace information for an ancestor working in a local shop, some department stores have relatively good archives although genealogical information might be limited. Co-op archives *www.archive.coop* are held in Manchester (visited by prior appointment) but local Co-operative groups often have records including apprenticeships in the CRO, see Discovery at TNA. The

University of Glasgow holds House of Fraser archives *www. housefraserarchive.ac.uk* although often short on individual personnel records.

Don't be too alarmed about scurrilous internet gossip claiming 'shop assistant' was a euphemism for prostitute (Chapter 3).

Bibliography and Further Reading

Cox, Pamela, and Hobley, Annabel, *Shopgirls: True Stories of Friendship, Hardship and Triumph from behind the Counter*, Arrow, 2015

Horn, Pamela, *Behind the Counter; Shop Lives from Market Stall to Supermarket*, Sutton, 2006

Masset, Claire, *Department Stores*, Shire, 2010

Winstanley, Michael J, *The Shopkeeper's World 1830–1914*, Manchester University Press, 1983

THEATRE AND MUSIC HALL

Not a respectable profession for women – and variety and music hall was the lower end of propriety. Male impersonators, women dressed as men performing risqué songs, were hugely popular from the 1890s until the end of the First World War, during which they were routinely involved in the conscription process. Music hall stars who made their living impersonating men include Hetty King (Winifred Emms, 1883–1972, no relation of mine) who followed her father into show business in 1905. The National Portrait Gallery *www.npg.org.uk* has ten portraits of her. 'Britain's Best Recruiting Sergeant' during the First World War was Vesta Tilley, another comedian's daughter, real name Matilda Alice Powles (1864–1952). Her signature song was 'Burlington Bertie'. American-born Ella Shields (Ella Buscher, 1879–1952) was equally famous for cross-dressing and performing 'Burlington Bertie'. All three married. Mainstream theatre was slightly more acceptable.

Although rare, there were female playwrights. Karl Marx's youngest daughter, unsuccessful actress Eleanor Marx Aveling (1855–98), translated plays and books including Ibsen's *The Lady from the Sea*, performed at Terry's Theatre, 1891, and Flaubert's *Madame Bovary*. Tragically, she committed suicide (poison, aged 43) after discovering the man she'd lived with for years, Edward Aveling, had married a younger actress. Other female nineteenth-century playwrights include poet Joanna Baillie (1762–1851), born in Scotland. Her several plays were performed at Drury Lane including one where the main role was played by legendary Edmund Kean. She never married. Jane Scott (c1779–1839) co-managed the Sans Pareil (later Adelphi) Theatre with her father and, before retiring to marry, had written more than fifty stage pieces by 1819.

The Victoria and Albert Museum *www.vam.ac.uk/page/m/music-hall* owns a large collection of ephemera and archives from variety and music hall (some transferred from the now-closed Theatre Museum, Covent Garden) as well as short online biographies of some stars. A music hall website dedicated to Arthur Lloyd (1839–1904) at *www.arthurlloyd.co.uk* contains over 1,500 pages and 12,000 archive images on the history of music hall and theatre in the UK and Ireland. Information includes theatres countrywide, many with historic photos and playbills etc. The largely donated archives at the British Music Hall Society *http://britishmusichallsociety.com* include song sheets, show cards, programmes, photographs and books; visits strictly by prior appointment. The Music Hall Guild of Great Britain and America *www.themusichallguild.com* is another charity dedicated to commemorating stars of the genre. They have an online alphabetical database with dates of birth, spouses, children and where they performed plus repertoire. Not all named artistes have information attached to them. Although centred on travelling showmen and circuses, there is a crossover with variety and music hall, therefore Sheffield University's National Fairground and Circus Archive *www.sheffield.ac.uk/nfca* may be of interest.

The University of Bristol holds the Mander and Mitchenson Collection of British Theatre ephemera *www.bristol.ac.uk/theatre-collection/ explore/theatre/mander—mitchenson-collection*. Its catalogue is online via their webpage. As some of its collection is held offsite, you're advised to make a prior appointment to view. Vesta Tilley's self-compiled scrap books are at Worcester County Record Office.

If an ancestor performed between 1806 and 1900, try the Adelphi Theatre Calendar, an American project (University of Massachusetts Amherst) recording the history of London's Sans Pareil/Adelphi Theatre (Pareil 1806–1819, Adelphi 1819–1900). Their website *www. umass.edu/AdelphiTheatreCalendar/actr.htm* includes authors, an attempt to name every actress (and actor) performing at the theatre and when. By cross-referencing dates with performance, it's possible to search for reviews and billings in contemporary newspapers.

You might find adverts and newspaper reviews especially in *The Examiner* (1808–81) and diurnal *The Morning Post* (1801–1900), both on subscription at British Newspaper Archive *www.british newspaperarchive.co.uk,* free at the British Library. Show business periodicals *The Stage* (from 1880) and, in direct competition, *The Era* are also at the BNA. Plays prior to 1834 are at Huntingdon Library California, searchable at the British Library Manuscripts Reading Room on microfiche: MS Fiche 253/1-1297 and MS Fiche 254/1-1070. You must be a registered reader (free) to access it. The British Library holds eighteen volumes of J P Wearing's *The London Stage: A Calendar of Plays and Players: 1890–1959* (Methuen, 1976–93).

The Examiner covered theatrical stories including obituaries, a section titled 'theatrical gossip' and reviews under 'Theatrical Examiner'. The *Morning Post* published theatre billings often naming actresses performing in a production, plus advertisements for singing and elocution teachers seeking pupils.

The British Library collections help-sheet is at *www.bl.uk/reshelp /findhelprestype/manuscripts/mssliterarytheatre/msslittheatre.html.* Remember, actresses often performed under stage names.

Perhaps the best resource is *Who's Who in the Theatre*, published 1922, now online at *https://archive.org/stream/bub_gb_qyk_ AQAA MAAJ#page/n7/mode/2up.* British and American actors are included with over 3,000 names in the obituary section, many from the nineteenth century. Opening with a theatrical directory, further chapters include biographies (e.g. actress Edith Cole, born 27 May

1870, names her father, husband and career précis); a separate continental biography includes Sarah Bernhardt (1844–1923); hereditary theatrical families; long runs in London theatres; notable productions; and an obituary section – albeit a list of names, e.g. actress Isabel Adams, aged 62, died 16 May 1893.

A case study of a postcard in my family album: 'Miss Daisy Irving. Appearing in "The Merry Widow" at Daly's Theatre'. With no message or stamp on the reverse, I resorted to Arthur Lloyd's webpage for Daly's Theatre which displays some fabulous contemporary photographs of the theatre in Cranbourne Street, Leicester Square (the site is now a cinema). Further down the webpage is a list of productions; eighteen in the twenty-eight years between 1898 and 1926 and, bingo, *The Merry Widow* ran for 1,107 performances in two productions, 18 June 1907 to 31 July 1909, revived 1923. *Who's Who in Theatre* reveals further gems. Irish-born actress and vocalist, Miss Irving married Lieutenant Colonel J Sargent of the Lancashire Fusiliers and appeared at

Daisy Irving, actress. Author's collection © Adèle Emm

Daly's from 9 June 1907 (discrepancy in dates) as Frou Frou in *The Merry Widow*. The entry lists her engagements up to 1919 including tours in America. Immigration records (via Ancestry) confirm the 'actress and singer' (her age varies) travelled unaccompanied first class (well done), to and from New York via Liverpool from 3 December 1910 through the First World War. As I couldn't find her in 1911, she may have been in the States on census day – or was she boycotting it? (See Chapter 6.)

Bibliography and Further Reading
Jackson, Russell, ed., *Victorian Theatre*, A&C Black, 1989
Powell, Kelly, *Women and Victorian Theatre*, Cambridge University
    Press, 2nd ed., 2008
Ruston, Alan R, *My Ancestor Worked in the Theatre*, Society of
    Genealogists, 2005

WASHERWOMEN, LAUNDRESSES AND CHARWOMEN
In 1851, stone mason George Spooner, wife Jane and his family lived in Pilsley, a Derbyshire village housing Chatsworth's estate workers. Ten years later, she's a widow supporting five children aged 7 to 20 (her eldest daughter had left home), surviving precariously hand to mouth as a charwoman. Charring was effectively work for the near destitute. In 1901, 111,841 women were recorded as charwoman, 86,463 of them married or widowed.

Charwomen were 'dailies', live-out servants, unlike washer-women and laundresses who worked from their own home, although some stately homes employed live-in laundry maids. Regarded as the most menial and lowest ranking servant, charwomen undertook odd jobs around the house; sewing and mending, light cleaning and dusting, laying the tablecloth, washing plates, toasting muffins and waiting at table until the servants had had their dinner or tea. They had an appalling reputation for light fingers and laziness.

The earliest recorded use of 'char' (*char/cherre/chore*, middle English meaning 'turn of work') is in the 1590s. An 1850 parody in *Punch* describes them aged 40 to 60, the 'lowest trade of domestic' wearing pattens (iron-soled wooden shoes), dirty mob-cap, battered black bonnet, soiled ribbons that, sun or rain, are never tied, a tucked-up gown, and bare arms 'of an unpleasant redness all the way up to the sleeve'. Earning about 1s 6d a day plus beer, tea and sugar (9s for a six-day week), it works out at about £39 a year living out, considerably more than live-in servants. The charwoman was notorious for smoking tobacco and taking snuff, and householders were advised to lock away tea caddies and count their silver spoons when she went home at night.

A large percentage of *laundresses and washerwomen* in censuses were widows; a considerable number ended their lives in the workhouse and pauper's grave. Taking in washing from other households, they washed laundry at home, later returning it. How did near destitute women (a) afford fuel and (b) soap, especially when subjected to soap tax (1712 to 1853)?

It must have been appallingly hard work especially for women living in small cramped houses where condensation dripped off walls. Some specialised in one element of the laundry like widowed Mrs Ford in Dover, 1882, who took in mangling. Bleaching and starching were other specialised tasks.

Washing took an entire day. On traditional washday, Monday, women boiled water on their fires from about five in the morning, then scrubbed and washed in a tub with dolly, mangled the wet clothes and finally put them out to dry often on communal lines strung across the street, hung in the back yard or even on bushes. Tuesday was ironing day. For anyone making her living as washerwoman, she must have worked all week bar, of course, Sunday.

Soap was produced from a mixture of lye (wood ash – acidic, very caustic) and tallow (animal fat). Imagine those red, raw hands! For those living where the plant soapwort could be obtained, it was turned into soap by chopping up stems and leaves and boiling the mixture for fifteen minutes before cooling and straining. This concoction was unsuitable for fine lace and linen. Local washerwomen only washed durable fabrics.

Solid soap was invented during the industrial revolution by chemists, many of whom made a fortune (e.g. Lydia Becker's father, Chapter 6). Pears was invented in 1789 (therefore subject to tax) by Cornish-born barber Andrew Pears, owner of a Soho shop. Sunlight Soap, invented in the 1880s, is arguably the most famous.

Advising middle-class households in 1861, Mrs Beeton explained the process so a housewife could supervise her servants. First clothes were separated, wool, linens, cotton, etc. washed by a different method; linens, for instance, were soaked overnight in soda and boiled for two hours the following day.

Washhouse and laundry, Victoria Baths, Manchester, 1906. This utilitarian building was behind the prestigious swimming baths. © Adèle Emm

Communal drying area behind houses in Withington, Manchester. © Adèle Emm

The first public washhouses were opened following the 1844 Washhouses Act and proliferated after the 1850 Public Baths and Wash-houses Act. Predictably, the first was the Frederick Street washhouse in London, 1842, rebuilt 1854. Although largely aimed at women living in cramped conditions, I'm sure many took advantage of public washhouses to wash clothes for other families. By the late 1880s, such washhouses were everywhere with facilities for washing, mangling, drying and ironing.

Some houses were built with communal areas behind them (commonly called 'crofts') used as drying areas for houses backing onto them still found, for instance, near Withington Hospital, Manchester.

Newspapers are full of reports of stolen washing. The *Bradford Observer*, 18 October 1892, reported Frank Connell, 17, having stolen two vests worth 9s property of Thomas Gosling of Newark Street, just after Gosling's wife had hung them in the passage. The youth received a month's jail with hard labour. Washing tubs were also frequently purloined. As reported in *Newcastle Courant*, Isabella M'Glaghan, 62, pleaded guilty to stealing a tub from Ann Smith on 24 October 1844. On 1 January 1845 Isabella received a month's prison sentence from Newcastle Winter Sessions. Had she hoped to earn a few coppers by taking in washing herself?

Laundry work was a rehabilitative pursuit in e.g. Industrial Schools (Chapter 2).

TRADE DIRECTORIES

Directories are useful for giving addresses between census records. Some are online but slow to navigate as many contain more than 1,000 pages. Not all years or areas have been digitised and local libraries, CROs and TNA have hard copies e.g. Post Office, Pigot and Kelly. Some areas had similar local publishers.

Some CROs have scanned trade directories for instance, Cheshire, at *http://cheshiredirectories.manuscripteye.com/index.htm* with

- 1822–3 Pigot's Directory of Cheshire
- 1857 Post Office Directory of Cheshire
- 1864 Morris & Co. Directory of Cheshire
- 1871 Worrall's Directory of Warrington
- 1878 Post Office Directory of Cheshire
- 1883 Slater's Directory of Cheshire and Liverpool
- 1895 Slater's Directory of Warrington, Widnes and St Helens
- 1902 Kelly's Directory of Cheshire
- 1906 Kelly's Directory of Cheshire
- 1910 Kelly's Directory of Cheshire

Take widowed Hannah Ambler, licensee of the Feathers in Stalybridge High Street. She's listed in the 1883 Slater's Directory, Cheshire and Liverpool, under Taverns and Public Houses. Retailers of Beer are listed separately. She's still there in 1891, aged 55, Pub Inn Keeper living with two nephews, both barmen, Frank and James

Buckley, and two servants. Having made a pretty penny from her trade, Hannah died in nearby Dukinfield, 5 March 1915, leaving an estate worth £4,683 4s 8d.

Leicester University has online directories covering the 1790s to the 1910s with free access to pdf files at *http://specialcollections. le.ac.uk/cdm/landingpage/collection/p16445coll4*. The University has entered into partnership with Ancestry which may make searches quicker. Some local historians have transcribed trade directories, for instance Neil Richardson of Tameside Family History at *http:// tamesidefamilyhistory.co.uk* has e.g. pages from *Manchester and Salford Trade Directory*, 1821/22.

In the unlikely event a female ancestor took on her husband's engineering trade or works, try Grace's Guide *www.gracesguide.co.uk* claiming to be the leading source of historical information on industry and manufacturing in Britain.

Bibliography and Further Reading

Andy Alston's Repository, Cotton Industry Jobs, *www.andrew alston.co.uk/cottonindustryjobs.html*

Baker, Richard Anthony, *British Music Hall: An Illustrated History*, Pen & Sword, 2014

Booth, Charles, et al., *Life and Labour of the People in London*, Macmillan, 1903, *https://archive.org/stream/lifeandlabourpe02 bootgoog/lifeandlabourpe02bootgoog_djvu.txt*

Cobbett, William, *Rural Rides*, A Cobbett, 1830

Emm, Adèle, *Tracing Your Trade and Craftsman Ancestors*, Pen & Sword, 2015

Engels, Friedrich, *The Condition of the Working Class in England*, 1845; trans. from German by Florence Kelley Wischnewetzky, William Reeves, 1888

Gaskell, Elizabeth, *North and South*, Chapman & Hall, 1855, novel about the textile industry

Hardy, Thomas, Far From the Madding Crowd, Smith, Elder & Co., 1874 novel: films 1967, 2015

Jackson, Lee, *Dictionary of Victorian London*, *www.victorianlondon.org*

Neff, Wanda, *Victorian Working Women: An Historical and Literary Study of Women in British Industries and Professions 1832–1850*, Cass, 1929

Parker, John, *Who's Who in the Theatre, A Biographical Record of the Contemporary Stage*, Boston, 1912 and 1922, *https://archive.org/details/bub_gb_qyk_AQAAMAAJ*

Parkes, R Bessie, *Essays on Women's Work*, Alexander Strahan, 1866

Ruston, Alan, *My Ancestors Worked in the Theatre*, Society of Genealogists, 2015

Shrimpton, Jayne, *British Working Dress, Occupational Clothing, 1715–1950*, Bloomsbury Shire, 2012

Tonna, Charlotte Elizabeth, *Helen Fleetwood*, R B Seeley & W Burnside, 1843, novel about female Manchester millworkers

UK Commissioners Report of Children's Employment, 1842, via Ancestry, *https://search.ancestry.co.uk/search/db.aspx?dbid= 34775*

Victorian Occupations websites, *www.census1891.com/occupations.php* and *http://rmhh.co.uk/occup/index.html*

Victorian Web, *www.victorianweb.org/victorian/history/work*

Vynne, Nora, and Blackburn, Helen, *Women under the Factory Act*, Norgate, 1903 (refers specifically to 1901 Factory and Workshops Act and includes working conditions in several occupations)

Ward, Margaret, *Women's Employment 1850–1950*, Countryside, 2008

Chapter 6

EMANCIPATION

We are here not because we are lawbreakers;
we are here in our efforts to be law makers.
(Emmeline Pankhurst, 1858–1928)

At the beginning of the nineteenth century, the majority of women had little say in their lives, their possessions and bodies legally belonged to their husband. Professions and universities were closed to them; many could barely read or write. By 1918, just over a century later, women had infiltrated universities, joined professions and some married women over 30 were allowed to vote. The metaphorical distance women had travelled was immense.

'Middling women' were not expected or encouraged to take paid employment, or approved of if they did. They were heavily discouraged from speaking in a public meeting and restricted in the meetings she could attend – usually at religious institutions. Amongst the first women known to address a public meeting was Catherine Booth (1829–90) preaching at her husband's Salvation Army congregation in June 1860.

As for a woman espousing political views; never! The universal view was she didn't have the education or intellectual acumen to vote. Without an education women were belittled by men, of whom the majority in the nineteenth century believed female education was an anathema, harmed their breeding capabilities and defeminised them. Education and enfranchisement go hand in hand. Mary Wollstonecraft's (1759–97) *A Vindication of the Rights of Women* (1792) was a response to Charles Maurice de Talleyrand-Perigord's 1791 report to the French Assembly arguing women should only receive a basic education.

Paradoxically, in the nineteenth century (as today), there were more women than men. 'Superfluous women' (an expression coined in April 1859 by Harriet Martineau (1802–76) in the *Edinburgh Review*) referred to the huge number of spinsters and widows who had minimal resources with which to survive. The term was revived after the slaughter of the First World War.

Of course women campaigned to change attitudes. The *Englishwoman's Review/English Woman's Journal*, published 1858–64, promoted women's employment and its quality, access to education and financial independence. The *Journal* was established in London by two well-connected women, Bessie Rayner Parkes Belloc (1828–1925, mother to poet Hilaire Belloc) and her friend, Barbara Leigh Smith Bodichon (1827–91), co-founder of Girton and Florence Nightingale's cousin.

Bodichon and Parkes worked from 19 Langham Place, London, a club for women where the reading room and coffee shop were open until ten at night. Launched December 1859 by Theodosia, Lady Monson (1803–91), it became a hotbed of women's professional and educational aspirations collectively known as the Langham Place Group/Circle, active until c1866. Members included familiar and influential names: educationalist Emily Davies (1830–1921); sisters Elizabeth and Millicent Garrett (later Anderson and Fawcett); editor and author Helen Blackburn (1842–1902) whose books and archives were bequeathed to Girton; novelist and part-time actress Matilda Mary Hays (1820–97); Emily Faithfull (1835–95) and Jessie Boucherett (1825–1910), founder of the Society for Promoting the Employment of Women (1859; archives at Girton) which, after several reincarnations, exists today as the charity Futures for Women.

Few of these women married, indeed several had lesbian affairs. Lady Monson's marriage to Frederick John Monson, 5th Baron Monson, reputedly lasted less than a week, with Matilda Hays becoming her companion in later years.

But such female campaigns were influencing enlightened men. John Stuart Mill, for instance, publicly questioned the lack of educational opportunities for women. His book, *The Subjection of*

Women, was published 1869, the same year as female ratepayers were allowed to vote in municipal elections. He was in the minority.

Women themselves did not universally champion the cause. Dissenters included Queen Victoria who denounced 'this mad, wicked folly of women's rights with all its attendant horrors' deterring women from 'the quiet paths of helpful, real work' (Octavia Hill, co-founder National Trust). The Women's Anti-Suffrage League, campaigning between 1907 and 1918, ironically included poet and writer Hilaire Belloc MP, son of feminist Bessie Rayner Parkes.

ENFRANCHISEMENT

The demand for enfranchisement (the right for women to vote or be given political privileges) was a countrywide phenomenon. In Manchester, self-educated daughter of a manufacturing chemist, Lydia Ernestine Becker (1827–90), finding herself excluded from all intellectual clubs because of her gender, vigorously campaigned for female enfranchisement.

It was unfair, the argument ran, that, although expected to pay rates and taxes, women couldn't vote for parliamentary representation which set those taxes. She was the first secretary of the Manchester Society for Women's Suffrage (1867) but another claim to fame is that she was amongst the earliest women orators countrywide to speak at public meetings attended by men. Initially facing ridicule and hostility, she insisted meetings had seats specifically reserved for women – a ground-breaking decision. By 1869, she was speaking on female franchise issues at prestigious venues such as Leeds Mechanics' Institute and Manchester's Free Trade Hall. Her stance provoked relentless male heckling and misogyny including a disgraceful *Ode* published in newspapers:

> Oh maiden with a charming name,
> But with a most uncomely mission,
> Why to the franchise lay a claim,
> When marriage should be your mission?
> (William Gaspey, Keswick, October 1868)

Opposition was dealt with scathing humour and fortitude; it's a shame she's largely been forgotten.

It was Lydia Becker who exhorted women to vote in the November 1867 Manchester by-election. The date is important; that year's Representation of the People Act enfranchised 'man' (an ambiguous term) fulfilling certain requirements including property ownership. According to lawyer Richard Pankhurst, Emmeline's husband, the argument was that *man*, a generic word, could signify *anyone* who owned property. As President of the Manchester Society, Lydia encouraged 7,000 property-owning Manchester women to claim a place on the electoral registers for the following year's 1868 general election.

However, two days before the 1867 November by-election, one woman's name accidently slipped onto the electoral register, that of Scottish-born widow Lilly/Lily Maxwell (born c1800), a Chorlton cum Medlock shop-owner. Casting a vote in those days was public (shouting your choice in front of others – men) thereby making it improper for women to attend polling stations. Lilly, notwithstanding, was enthusiastic and, accompanied by Lydia and another female committee member, predictably voted for Jacob Bright, a supporter of women's suffrage (he won).

The following year, all rate-paying women who submitted their names for inclusion on the electoral roll had to have their application approved by a male revising barrister. The majority were rejected apart from a few in Manchester and a handful in Lydiate, Ormskirk, whose barrister, Thomas Chisholm Anstey, was sympathetic to universal suffrage. Although thirteen women's names crept onto Manchester's electoral register for the 1868 general election, only nine, supported by Lydia Becker, had the courage to vote.

There were two victims in this election. John Stuart Mill, the indispensable champion of female suffrage, lost his Westminster seat to W H Smith of newspaper distribution fame – and female suffrage in general elections was declared illegal.

SUFFRAGISTS AND SUFFRAGETTES

Lydia would have called herself a *suffragist*, a movement dating from the 1850s when women, barred from public speaking, encouraged influential men to espouse and promote their cause. Suffragists supported similar feminist issues like equal pay or Josephine Butler's campaign to decriminalise prostitution. Bastions of the suffragist crusade founded organisations like the London Society of Women's Suffrage (from 1865) and its Manchester branch. In November 1897, under the presidency of Millicent Fawcett, seventeen regional societies became members of an umbrella organisation, the NUWSS (National Union of Women's Suffrage Societies). The minutes for this inaugural meeting are on the Living Heritage site *www. parliament.uk/about/living-heritage/transformingsociety/electionsvoting/ womenvote/unesco/nuwss-foundation.* By 1913, the NUWSS included nearly 500 groups nationwide including the Women's Freedom League (1907) and Actresses Franchise League (1908).

At the turn of the twentieth century, the campaign for women's enfranchisement gained momentum – everyone recognises one name. Emmeline Pankhurst's breakaway group, the notorious WSPU (Women's Social and Political Union) founded 1903, made headlines and garnered publicity – much of it extremely negative. These were the *suffragettes*; the militants whose mantra was 'Deeds

Emmeline Pankhurst's blue plaque, Manchester.

not Words' and who prohibited men joining their organisation. It was these who staged increasingly violent and infamous tactics: chaining themselves to railings (from 1908), hurling bricks through shop windows, attacking paintings in public art galleries (Manchester, 1913), slashing Velazquez's *Rokeby Venus* in the National Gallery (1914). They went on hunger strike in prison and their force-feeding initiated the Cat and Mouse Act, 1913, providing temporary release for ill health. Some Cat and Mouse Act documents held in the Parliamentary Archives (HL/PO/PU/1/1913/3&4G5c4) can be viewed on *www.parliament.uk/about/living-heritage/ transformingsociety/electionsvoting/womenvote/case-study-the-right-to-vote/the-right-to-vote/winson-green-forcefeeding/cat-and-mouse-act*. At the declaration of war in 1914, the WSPU suspended action to help the war effort.

Former Manchester home of Emmeline Pankhurst and her family. Now the Pankhurst Centre. © Adèle Emm

A major issue for anyone researching a suffragette (or suffragist) ancestor is the boycott of the 2 April 1911 census. Under the slogan 'No vote, No census' many stayed away overnight. Paradoxically, if your ancestor doesn't appear, you could deduce she supported votes for women . . .

The Women's Library founded 1866 held at the LSE is the pre-eminent archive for the suffragist and women's movement *www. lse.ac.uk/Library/Collections/Collection-highlights/The-Womens-Library.* It owes its origin to suffragette (WSPU) Ruth Cavendish -Bentinck née St Maur (1867–1953) whose collection of over 1,000 books was donated, 1918, to the NUWSS. The Woman's Library also holds her archives and papers, plus those of the National Anti-Suffrage League, the Pankhursts, Millicent Fawcett and her eponymous Society *www.fawcettsociety.org.uk.* FindMyPast has a Suffragette Collection *www.findmypast.co.uk/suffragette-collection.*

Another resource is London's Bishopsgate Institute *http://www. bishopsgate.org.uk/library* whose collections include feminist and women's history with accounts of suffragette activity in e.g. Twickenham and Greenwich. Ancestry has the Index of Women Arrested 1906–1914 but details are sparse – name, date of arrest and where – however, you'll have confirmed an ancestor was suffragette not suffragist. Also try CROs.

The Women' Suffrage Movement Collection is on open access on microfilm (M50/1/1-1/2 1-98) at Manchester Central Library. It holds key archives of the Parliamentary Committee for Women's Suffrage (1892–1903); the Manchester Men's League for Women's Suffrage (1909–18); the National Union of Women's Suffrage Societies (1910–14) and the International Woman Suffrage Alliance (1913–20). The catalogue by Adam Matthew Publications lists what each microfilm contains including minutes, correspondence and papers from and received by Lydia Becker, the Manchester Society for Women's Suffrage, and Millicent Garrett Fawcett etc. The National Union of Women's Suffrage Societies Archive is held by the University of Manchester Library at John Rylands.

The People's History Museum in Manchester has a help-sheet

People's History Museum, Manchester. © Adèle Emm

for women's suffrage at *www.phm.org.uk/wp-content/uploads/ 2011/10/7-Womens-suffrage.pdf.* The National Archives help-sheet is *www.nationalarchives.gov.uk/help-with-your-research/research-guides/ womens-suffrage.* Archives mainly cover the period from 1905 to the First World War. Contemporary newspapers are another resource.

ELECTORAL REGISTERS AND BURGESS ROLLS

A *burgess* was an inhabitant of a town or borough entitled to vote in local elections and could include Freemen of a city or borough. They predate the 1832 parliamentary Reform Act providing a vote to all householders (as long as they were male) who paid a yearly rental of £10 or more. 'Burgess Rolls' is therefore another name for an electoral register so, until the 1869 Act, you're unlikely to find a female ancestor listed.

The vast majority of names in the Stockport Burgess Rolls for 1 November 1869 to 1 November 1870 were men; the first two pages comprised about ninety names with eight being women. Information includes: full name, type of property and address. Harriet Barber of 4 Heron Street, Edgeley ward, was eligible to vote. The 1871 census (as Herrons Street), reveals Harriot (sic) Barber, 60, single, employed in bleach-works.

Ancestry holds electoral registers for several regions including East Riding of Yorkshire, Kingston in Surrey and London for 1832–1965. In some, women are in separate sections from men e.g. Ulleskelfe Polling District in Yorkshire's East Riding (1890). Try locally; for instance, a 126 page guide to Staffordshire electoral registers 1832–2001, lists what survives and where *www. staffordshire.gov.uk/leisure/archives/services/publications/ERguideWeb versionApr2010.pdf.* Some are on microfilm.

Electoral registers were compiled, depending on area, once a year so it's possible to trace addresses between censuses. Information includes address; whether accommodation was furnished or unfurnished; amount of rent payable. The British Library has the national collection of printed electoral registers from when they were first produced under the Representation of the People Act 1832 to the present day and, at the time of writing, are working with FindMyPast, to digitise them; *www.bl.uk/collection-guides/uk-electoral-registers.* TNA has a small collection from the 1870s.

Under the Local Government Act, 1888, female rate-payers could be registered to vote for county councillors. A token example from Ulleskelf, 1890, confirms their franchise status 'Occupation Voters (other than lodgers) Division Three, Persons entitled to vote as County Electors but not as Parliamentary Voters' and the first four women, all living in cottages in Kirkby Wharfe, are Harriet Birdsall, Hannah Dean, Ann Harris and Jane Tindal. In 1891, Pocklington-born widow and laundress Harriet Birdsall, 60, (yes, low-status women could now vote in county elections) lived with her son, 25, and two grandchildren. Did she take advantage of her vote?

A more likely advocate was Miss Rhoda Fysh, who, in 1891 aged

46, was Principal of Kingston High School for Girls (later Tiffin Girls' School; Rhoda Ward Fysh was its first headmistress when it opened in 1879). Two years earlier she appears in the Surrey Electoral Register living in London Road, Kingston. In 1906, she paid Poor Rate (rental value £36 per annum) for property in Northfield, Birmingham, alongside housemate, another spinster and girls' school principal, Bessie Davis. In 1911, the two shared their property on 'independent means'. No census boycotting for them ... In 1913, Bessie left her estate to lifelong partner Rhoda and her will includes some genealogical background.

If education was key to female emancipation, employment, access to professions and enfranchisement, effective teachers were required. Female teachers.

TEACHER TRAINING

Amongst the earliest colleges founded to train female teachers was Whitelands, Putney (1841, now luxury apartments) by the Church of England's National Society and it predates all English universities apart from Oxford, Cambridge, London and Durham. Another offering higher education to women was Queen's College, London, founded 1848 (Chapter 2).

Before 1870, a headmaster could supervise training under the pupil-teacher training system. Such teachers were generally inferior so, following the Education Act 1870, separate establishments were created. Several well-known women's teacher training colleges were inaugurated around this time including Maria Grey College (Teachers' Training and Registration Society College, 1878, renamed 1886), Froebel (1892) and England's first non-denominational college, Edge Hill, Liverpool (1885). From 1902, pupil-teacher training was further tightened. The TNA's teacher training help-sheet is at *www.nationalarchives.gov.uk/help-with-your-research/research-guides/teacher-training.*

Schools and colleges are often included in local directories occasionally naming teachers and subjects. FindMyPast has Teacher's Registration Council Registers (1914–48) for nearly 100,000 teachers working in English and Welsh schools 1870–1948, half of them women. Information might include name (occasionally maiden names for married teachers), date of registration and register number, the school's address, attainments, experience and where they trained.

Derek Gillard's Education in England website at *www.education england.org.uk/history* is a useful overview.

TEACHERS' UNIONS

Coinciding with the Education Act, the National Union of Elementary Teachers was founded in June 1870 with 400 members when, under the Revised Code, teachers' pay was commensurate with pupils' results. The Union's intention was to campaign against this plus improve pay, conditions, status and state education. In 1888, it became the National Union of Teachers (NUT) and by 1910 had over 68,000 members. The first teachers' strike was in 1896. As usual, committee members were predominantly male but, at the Annual Teachers' Conference, 1896, held in Brighton as reported in *South Wales Daily News*, 8 April, Annie Salvage was the elected representative for Lincoln.

Archives for the NUT (now National Education Union) are at Bishopsgate Institute with a summary of its collection at *www. bishopsgate.org.uk/content.aspx?CategoryID=1519.* For the NUT and photographic catalogue, try *www.bishopsgate.org.uk/uploads/media/ 98/10648.pdf.*

UNIVERSITIES

For ambitious women to become doctors and lawyers, they first had to be admitted to university – strenuously denied them for one reason only. Gender. When archaeologist, traveller and Middle East cartographer Gertrude Bell (1868–1926) attended St Margaret's Hall, Oxford, in the mid-1880s (reading history, one of the limited subjects available to women) one lecturer forced female students to sit with their backs facing him rather than see their faces. Gertrude Bell, incidentally, was anti-suffrage.

Girton College, Cambridge *www.girton.cam.ac.uk* was founded in 1869 with five female students. By 1871, twelve shared a house in Hitchin, Hertfordshire, and, because the house was too small, relocated to Girton, 1873, under its Mistress (and suffragist) Emily Davies. That year, they took the first Cambridge Tripos examinations but, although everyone passed, didn't matriculate. Why not?

Although they could study and sit final examinations, they weren't awarded the degree! So impassioned against female students were they that, in 1897 following months of heated debate and demonstrations, male Cambridge students celebrated all night when women were still denied matriculation.

Slade School of Art, London, was the first to accept women on the same fine art course as men, 1871. London University was the first admitting female students for undergraduate degrees, 1878. The first Oxford colleges for women were Lady Margaret Hall (1878) and Somerville (1879). However, although Annie Mary Henley Rogers achieved first-class honours in Latin and Greek at Oxford in 1877, she only matriculated half a century later, 26 October 1920, alongside other women also refused prior matriculation.

Scotland was more progressive with the first women graduating from Edinburgh University in 1894; their first female doctors graduated 1896.

The first female professor, Edith Morley (1875–1964), was appointed in 1908 at what is now Reading University. She taught English language.

It was only in 1921 that Cambridge saw fit to confer degrees but no other privileges to women and it took another twenty years, 1948, for women to receive them with the full status conferred. Indeed, women sat in a separate examination hall until the 1950s.

Generally speaking, university records are held at the university. London University alumni 1836–1945 are on Ancestry; just date and subject. FindMyPast has some records for Oxford and Cambridge but although Cambridge University Alumni 1261–1900 are on Ancestry, women's colleges aren't included. Girton College Register 1869–1946 was published privately and is held in the College's

Archives and Special Collections; *www.girton.cam.ac.uk/library/ archive-and-special-collections.* Prearranged appointments are required.

If taking a classics or mathematics degree was one hurdle, becoming a doctor was akin to climbing Everest.

THE PROFESSIONS
For nursing, see Chapter 5.

The traditional three professions are law, medicine and the church. The first female solicitor, Carrie Morrison (1888–1950) was appointed in December 1922, the same year the first woman was elected to the Royal Academy of Arts (Annie Swynnerton, 1844–1933). The Church of England appointed its first female priests 12 March 1994.

The battle for women to become doctors began in the mid-nineteenth century.

Doctors
The first woman cited as a doctor in England, although masquerading as a man to do so, was Margaret Ann Bulkely (1792/5–1865) under the guise of military surgeon James Barry. Born in South Africa, she arrived in Edinburgh under her pseudonym and trained at its medical school graduating 1812. After a six months' stint at St Thomas' Hospital, London, she became an army surgeon and, like Florence Nightingale, was convinced surgical success was attributable to good hygiene and diet. It was only after her death that Barry was revealed to have been a woman.

America's first female doctor was Bristol-born Elizabeth Blackwell (1821–1910) who emigrated as a child and graduated top of her class from Geneva Medical College, New York, in 1849. Returning to England in 1869, she and Florence Nightingale opened a women's medical college. By now, having been influenced by Blackwell's example, England had its first female doctor, Elizabeth Garrett Anderson (1836–1917), sister to suffragist Millicent Fawcett née Garrett. Battling male prejudice, Elizabeth qualified as an

Elizabeth Garrett Anderson Hospital, Euston Road, London. Originally New Hospital for Women renamed 1918. © Adèle Emm

apothecary in 1865. Her medical degree was awarded to her in Paris but the British Medical Register still stubbornly refused to admit her as a doctor. Only in 1876 with the passing of the Medical Act were women finally licensed.

Sophia Jex-Blake (1840–1922) was another pioneer of female clinicians and surgeons. Also inspired by Elizabeth Blackwell, she decided her vocation was in medicine and, believing Edinburgh medical school more enlightened than elsewhere, applied in 1876. However, because she was the only women registered on the course, the university declared it too expensive to teach her on her own. Responding to a newspaper article, more women enrolled. The 'Edinburgh Seven' as they became known, consisted of Isabel Thorne (née Pryer), Edith Pechey, Matilda Chaplin, Helen Evans, Mary Anderson and Emily Bovell. It didn't go well. Greeted with scorn and hostility, they were pelted with mud at lectures and the vanguard moved to London or France to complete their studies. Their achievements are impressive. Sophia Jex-Blake ran the London School of Medicine for Women 1874–77, opening the Edinburgh equivalent in 1877 (closed 1898). For a year, she established and ran the Edinburgh Hospital and Dispensary for Women. Edith Pechey moved abroad and was ultimately appointed to India's University of Bombay senate. Although Isabel Thorne never fully qualified as a doctor, she became honorary secretary at the London School of Medicine for Women and in 1905 published its history, *A Sketch of the Foundation and Development of the London School of Medicine for Women*. However, her daughter, Mary Thorne (1861–1951), who never married, became a fully qualified physician and surgeon.

A history of medical women is found at *www.sciencemuseum. org.uk/broughttolife/themes/practisingmedicine/women* and *www.medical womensfederation.org.uk/about-us/our-history*.

Based on the annually published list of doctors licensed to practise in the UK and abroad, the General Medical Council Records, 1859–1959, are on Ancestry. They include the doctor's residence, qualification and date of registration. Women appear post the 1876 Medical Act.

The 1880 listing for Edinburgh Seven's Mary Edith Pechey reveals her at '4 Warwick Villas, Leeds, MD Bern 1877, LKQCP Ireland and LM 1877; (Univ. and Surg. Hall Edin., Lond Sch for Wom. and Univ of Bern); Lects on Hygiene Lond Sch of Med for Wom; late House Surg Birm and Midld. Hosp. for Wom.' It does not reveal her battle to get there.

Dentists

The first woman with a British qualification in dentistry (1895) was Lilian Lindsay née Murray (1871–1960). Educated at Camden School for Girls (founded by our friend Frances Buss, Chapter 2), she graduated from the Royal College of Surgeons, Edinburgh, 3 May 1895, licensed 20 May. A blue plaque commemorates her life and achievements at 2 Hungerford Road, Holloway; *www.english-heritage.org.uk/visit/blue-plaques/lindsay-lilian-1871-1960*. Unlike many professional women of her time, Lilian married.

Until relatively recently, dentistry was not a popular career for women, however, if you do have a female dentist in your family history, Ancestry has Dentist Registers 1879–1942 courtesy of the Wellcome Library. Lindsay's 1910 entry lists her address (2 Brandon Street, Edinburgh), date of registration and qualifications.

BUSINESS WOMEN

In a world dominated by men when female education was given low priority, it's hard to find examples of female entrepreneurs other than shop keepers and widows continuing a husband's business, especially before 1882.

A rare and early example is Madame Vestris (1797–1856), the first woman to lease a theatre in London's West End – or indeed anywhere. This English-born daughter of European immigrants married a French dancer at 16, but, deserted four years later, retained his surname for professional reasons. With such inauspicious beginnings, she invested the capital from her stage career first in the Olympic Theatre, 1831 (presenting burlesques and other extravaganzas). She later took on the Theatre Royal Covent Garden (manager in *A Swells' Night Guide*, 1841) and the Lyceum, one of the most popular theatres in London – still performing as she did so. With a reputation for on-stage propriety, she prevented louche behaviour from her male clientele towards the dancing girls, although the anonymous author of *A Swell's Night Guide* hinted, 'The private boxes of this theatre have snug and secret retiring anti-rooms with voluptuous couches, and all things requisite for the comfort and relaxation of the debauchée.' In 1851 (HO107/1469/65/15), she's recorded under her second husband's name, Eliza Lucia Matthews, as 'comedian'. According to the *National Dictionary of Biography*, 1882, her legacy was 'many improvements in stage scenery and effects'. A snide aside adds 'scandalous memoirs, published in   1839 for the booksellers, are untrustworthy in the main'. With rudimentary education, it's even more remarkable she was so successful.

You may find businesswomen listed in local directions and advertisements for their company in local newspapers. Grace's Guide *www.gracesguide.co.uk*, covering British industrial history, is another suggestion. Mary Broadbent and Son, for instance, was an Oldham cotton spinning company.

CIVIC DUTIES
If professions were denied women, there were other activities through which she could involve herself. Before 1869 (after which she could serve on a school board or act as Poor Law Guardian), philanthropic, humanitarian and altruistic duties were all that were open to her. These offered a bridge and experience towards later involvement in activism and local government. Such women tended to be the more educated, socially aware middle class.

Parish
The 1834 Poor Law Act enabled qualified women to vote for Poor Law Guardians, only for the right to be removed the following year until reinstated under the 1869 Municipal Franchise Act. As always, because subject content (poverty, criminal behaviour, etc.) was perceived as unsuitable for genteel women, many men disapproved.

The first elected female Poor Law Guardian (Kensington, 1875) was London-born spinster and language teacher Martha Crawford Merington/Merrington (1831–1912). By 1880, there were eight female Poor Law Guardians; 900 by 1895. A Poor Law Guardian's role was to administer workhouses, elect nurses, female servants and oversee housekeeping, clothing and education for girls in institutions.

School boards
The 1870 Education Act permitted women to vote and serve on school boards and many social crusaders took advantage. Scottish social reformer Flora Stevenson (1839–1905) is one. Lydia Becker proudly records it as her occupation in 1871. She was amongst the

earliest women countrywide to lay a foundation stone, her first at a girls' school in Burgess Street, Harpurhey (since demolished). Other familiar names elected to school boards include Annie Besant (Chapter 5), educationalist Emily Davies and doctor Elizabeth Garrett Anderson, with Garrett Anderson winning more votes (Marylebone) than any other candidate in the country. J W Walton's painting, *The First London School Board, 1870*, hangs at the Guildhall Art Gallery, London, and depicts the indomitable Davies and Anderson surrounded by men.

Local councils and councillors

The Municipal Franchise Act, 1869, gave a vote in local elections to women rate payers over the age of 21. However, the only women who could take advantage of this before 1882 were widows and spinsters; even then, she couldn't stand as councillor.

Following the 1888 County Councils Act which, amongst others, established the London County Council, two women stood as candidates; Margaret Mansfield, Lady Sandhurst, for Brixton and Jane Cobden (daughter of free-trader and Liberal statesman Richard Cobden) for Bow and Bromley. Both were successful. However, defeated, slighted and piqued male Brixton Conservative candidate, Beresford Hope, went to court and won the case because his opponent was a woman. Lady Sandhurst was fined £5 for every vote secured whilst serving on the Council. At the end of their tenure as councillors, neither woman was permitted to stand again. The following year, Lady Sandhurst was elected President of the Society for Promoting the Return of Women as County Councillors (renamed 1893 as the Women's Local Government Society). The aim? To promote women in local politics.

The Local Government Act, 1894, permitted all parish rate-payers, including women, to vote in parish elections. Some took the opportunity to serve on them as well. In a fit of sardonic humour, Charlotte Carmichael Stopes' 1894 book, *British Freewomen, their Historical Privilege, https://archive.org/stream/britishfreewomen00stopuoft* named women throughout British history (tellingly mainly medieval) who held powerful offices in order to decide, in a historical context, which women should have been awarded the vote!

From 1907, the Qualification of Women Act permitted women to sit as councillors, aldermen, mayors and chairman (no chair or chairperson in those days). In the 1907 Oldham by-election, Mrs Constance E Lees was amongst the first women elected onto a council. The first female mayor was our friend Dr Elizabeth Garrett Anderson, elected 1908 for Aldeburgh, Suffolk, following the death of husband James.

She wasn't the only familiar name taking advantage of civic duties. Emmeline Pankhurst was a Poor Law Guardian as was fellow suffragist and social reformer Charlotte Despard née French (1844–1939) who later stood for election for Battersea North, 1918.

WELFARE COMMITTEES AND GOOD WORKS

Here was another public sphere where a Victorian woman could expend spare energy, appease her social conscience and attempt to improve a woman's lot.

The Charity Commission was founded 1853 and its Minute Books are held at TNA. Women supported appropriate charities, i.e. preventing cruelty to children or aiding impoverished women when lying-in. Charities published annual reports. Although the majority of officials were prominent local men, if a woman were involved, she might be named. Remember, a married woman was recorded as Mrs without her Christian name.

The First Annual Report for the Liverpool Society for the Prevention of Cruelty for Children founded April 1883 was published March 1884 (held at TNA HO34 9547/5934). Its second page headed by the President (the male Mayor of Liverpool) lists the Society's Officers. At the very bottom, the Ladies' Committee names eleven women headed by their President, Lady Mary Eleanor Forwood, (née Moss, 1841–96), daughter of a Liverpudlian shipping magnate. The Committee consisted of Mrs Agnew, Digby Smith, Imlach, Goldie, Louis, Hibbert Taylor and Forrer (Honorary Secretary) accompanied by Misses Mary Stanistreet, Gregson and Davies.

By cross-checking the male committee, it's possible to marry up some members. The Chairman, T Fredk A Agnew Esq's commercial address is 5 Exchange Buildings (Liverpool's Cotton Exchange). In the 1891 census, he and wife Julia (born East Indies c1843) live elsewhere.

The report's last pages list Society donors and subscribers including the aforementioned Mrs J H Goldie (revealing her husband's initials) and a Miss Gregson both donating £10. Henry Forrer, presumably the husband of committee member Mrs Forrer, donated £1. The Agnews donated £10 plus an annual subscription of £2. Amongst the subscribers to the Liverpool Society is a girls' school listed under the name of a teacher. As today, children were encouraged to support local charities and, starting young, these girls would have come from wealthy homes.

Another example, the Co-operative Women's Guild, founded 1883 by Lady Alice Acland née Cunningham (1849–1939) and teacher Mary Lawrenson, provided educational and recreation facilities for women and girls. Campaigning on health and suffrage issues, this society was influential in the inclusion of maternity benefits in the 1911 National Insurance Act. Its archives are at the Bishopsgate Institute.

Finding an ancestor's name amongst charity benefactors or committees is unlikely to reveal genealogical information but it proves they either had a social conscience or, like the Pankhursts, were ambitious for social inclusion.

DORCAS SOCIETY

Named after Dorcas, a biblical woman who helped the poor, the aim of this society, founded in the Isle of Man 1834, was to provide clothes for impoverished members of the local community. Branches proliferated countrywide. The Glasgow branch, founded, 1864, by spinster and philanthropist Beatrice Clugston (1827–88) donated clothing to patients after leaving hospital. Few archives survive and those that do are held locally; for instance, the Bellahouston Dorcas Society minute book, 1885–1910, is held at the National Archives for

Scotland. Some records for the Bury Branch (founded 1885) are held amongst Bury's Bank Street Unitarian Church archives.

CLOTHING

Middle-class women's fashionable clothing preserved a woman's feminine demeanour and behaviour. For those in the lower echelons of society, her wardrobe was a matter of expediency. Working-class women wore what was available and for those toiling outdoors, they may have dressed in men's attire for practicality and durability.

American Amelia Bloomer née Jenks (1818–94) initiated the fashion for bloomers, acknowledging she didn't invent them. Known in the 1850s as 'Turkish dress', this sartorial elegance was ridiculed by the contemporary press, therefore women who wore trousers were those prepared to shock friends, relatives and colleagues. The style became associated with the feminist movement.

Charlotte Carmichael Stopes (1840–1929, mother of birth control advocate, Marie) campaigned against women's restrictive support garments but Lydia Becker in 1889 defended them as 'absolutely necessary for the health, comfort and appearance of women'. Perhaps Lydia was biased; she'd always suffered a bad back.

The Boy Scout movement was founded in 1907 by Robert Baden Powell (1857–1941). He published *Scouting for Boys* in 1908, and, in response to girls turning up at a 1909 Scout rally, the Girl Guide movement was formed 1910. They wore a feminised version of the boys' uniform. The Girl Guide Association archives *www.girl guiding.org.uk* are currently being curated.

PLACES TO VISIT

Pankhurst Centre, 60-62 Nelson Street, Manchester, M13 9WP
  (next to Manchester Royal Infirmary),
  www.thepankhurstcentre.org.uk
People's History Museum, Left Bank, Spinningfields, Manchester
  M3 3ER. Archives include Women's Labour League records,
  1906–18, *www.phm.org.uk*
Working Class Movement Library, 51 Crescent, Salford, M5 4WX,
  www.wcml.org.uk

Bibliography and Further Reading

Many books have been published on women's suffrage. I've included a representative sample.

Appleton, William, *Madame Vestris and the London Stage*, Columbia, 1974

Blackburn, Helen, *A Handbook for Women Engaged in Social and Political Work*, J W Arrowsmith, 1881

Blackburn, Helen, *Women's Suffrage: A Record of the Women's Suffrage Movement in the British Isles, with Biographical Sketches of Miss Becker,* Williams & Norgate, 1902

Blackburn, Helen, and Boucherett, Jessie, *The Condition of Working Women and the Factory Acts,* Elliot Stock, 1896

Blackburn, Helen, and Vynne, Nora, *Women under the Factory Act,* Williams & Norgate, 1903

Brittain, Vera, *Testament of Youth,* Gollancz, 1933

Common Cause, 1909–33, suffrage journal, BNA

Crawford, Elizabeth, *The Women's Suffrage Movement: A Reference Guide 1866–1928,* Routledge, 2000

Fawcett, Millicent Garrett, *Women's Suffrage, A Short History of a Great Movement,* T C & E C Jack, 1888, *www.gutenberg.org/files/48614/48614-h/48614-h.htm*

Fawcett, Millicent Garrett, *What I Remember,* Fisher Unwin, 1929

Fawcett, Millicent Garrett, *The Women's Victory and After, Personal Reminiscences 1911–1918,* Sidgwick & Jackson, 1920, *www.gutenberg.org/files/48833/48833-h/48833-h.htm*

Hollis, Patricia, *Ladies Elect, Women in English Local Government 1865–1914,* Clarendon Press, 1989

Housego, Molly, and Storey, Neil R, *The Women's Suffrage Movement,* Bloomsbury Shire, 2012

Kelly, Audrey, *Lydia Becker and the Cause,* Centre for North-West Regional Studies at the University of Lancaster, 1992

Meeres, Frank, *Suffragettes: How Britain's Women Fought and Died for the Vote,* Amberley, 2014

Mill, John Stuart, *The Subjection of Women,* Longmans, 1869

Morley, Edith, and Morris, Barbara, *Before and After: Reminiscences of a Working Life,* Two Rivers Press, 2016

Pankhurst, Emmeline, *Suffragette, My Own Story,* 1914; Vintage, 2015, *www.gutenberg.org/files/34856/34856-h/34856-h.htm*

Parker, Joan, 'Lydia Becker: Pioneer Orator of the Women's Movement', *Manchester Region History Review,* 5/2 (Autumn/ Winter 1991–2)

Robinson, Jane, *Hearts and Minds: The Untold Story of the Great Pilgrimage and How Women Won the Vote,* Doubleday, 2018

Rubenstein, David, *A Different World for Women. The Life of Millicent Garret Fawcett,* Harvester Wheatsheaf, 1991

Smith, Harold L, *The British Women's Suffrage Campaign, 1866– 1928,* 2nd ed., Longman, 2010

Smith, Sydney, *Enfranchisement of Women, the Law of the Land,* Trübner & Co., 1879

Stopes, Charlotte Carmichael, *British Freewomen: Their Historical Privilege,* Swan Sonnenschein, 1894, *https://archive.org/details/britishfreewomen00stopuoft*

Strachey, Ray, *The Cause,* G Bell & Sons, 1928

Tomalin, Claire, *The Life and Death of Mary Wollstonecraft,* Penguin, 2012

TIMELINE

1753   Marriage Act: all marriages to be conducted by a minister in a parish church or chapel and legally binding. Prevented illegal marriages prevalent in the 1740s and ensured anyone under 21 had parent's or guardian's permission. Nonconformists and Catholics to be married in Anglican Church. Remained in force until 1836

1801   First national census: out of a total population of 8.3 million in England, women outnumber men by 400,000

1802   Health and Morals of Apprentices Act: all apprentices under 21 prevented from working at night or longer than a twelve-hour day; apprentices to receive basic education. No enforcement

1803   Ellenborough Act: abortion prohibited, punishable by death. Amended 1837 and 1861

1816   First infant school (more a child-minding service) established by Robert Owen (1771–1858) at Lanarkshire for cotton mill workers' children aged 2 and above

1819   Cotton Mills and Factory Acts: illegal to employ children under 9; working hours limited to sixteen a day for under 16s. Inadequate enforcement; only two prosecutions by 1825

1820   Whipping Act: abolished flogging female prisoners

1823   Judgement of Death Act: judges given discretion to reduce mandatory death sentences to imprisonment or transportation (other than treason or murder); death sentence still recorded

1828   Offences Against the Person Act: repealed and simplified English law offence of petty (petit) treason, i.e. betrayal by a subordinate (e.g. wife or servant) to a superior (husband or employer). Under this Act until 1841, rape still carried the death penalty as did 'carnal knowledge' of girls under 10

1829   Governesses Mutual Assurance Society founded, followed
        by Governesses Benevolent and Provident Association
        (1841) and Governesses Benevolent Institution (1843)
        providing assistance and annuities to impoverished
        governesses

1831   Factory Act limited working day to twelve hours for those
        under 18. No enforcement. Wool and jute industries
        unaffected

1832   Great Reform Act excluded women from electorate by
        defining voters as 'male persons'

1833   Factory Act included wool factories. Maximum working
        week of forty-eight hours for those aged 9 to 13,
        maximum eight hours a day. For those between 13 and 18,
        hours limited to twelve a day. Compulsory elementary
        schooling of two hours a day for children under 13. Four
        male inspectors employed to enforce regulations for over
        4,000 mills

1834   Poor Law Amendment Act stopped outdoor relief (briefly
        reinstated in Lancashire during Cotton Famine 1861–5).
        Relief only available in the workhouse although in reality
        continued to be paid outside at reduced levels

1835   Lord Lyndhurst's Act: marriages to deceased wife's sister
        'null and void'

1836   Registration of Birth Marriage and Death Act(s): from July
        1837 births, marriages and deaths recorded by the state

1836   Marriage Act: Nonconformists and Catholics could
        marry in own place of worship.
        Register Offices established in towns and cities for non-
        religious civil marriages

1839   Custody of Infants Act: mothers could petition courts for
        custody of children under 7 and access to older children.
        See 1873

1840   Census Act: recorded everyone's details on a specific
        date enabling accurate demographic
        study of the population. First census in this format, 6 June

1841. Subsequent censuses every ten years except 1941

1842 Mines and Collieries Act banned women, girls and boys under 10 working underground

1844 Ragged School Union Act set up ragged schools countrywide

1844 Factory Act. Dangerous machinery fenced off; no child or young person to clean machinery whilst in motion; children limited to a six and a half hour day with three hours schooling; twelve-hour day for women and young people aged 13–18 with one and a half hours for meals; deaths and accidents at work to be reported to surgeons; half-time employment permitted for children 8 to 13

1845 Calico Print Works Act applied to factories printing on cotton fabrics: prohibited children under 8; no work between 10 p.m. and 6 a.m. for women and children under 13; children under 13 to attend school thirty days per half year. Did not apply to other industries

1847 Factories Act: 'Ten Hour Act' restricted women and children under 18 to a ten-hour day. Anomalies in Act tightened by subsequent legislation

1848 First college for women, Queen's, founded in London's Harley Street, initially training teachers

1851 Sheffield Female Political Association formed. Presented petition for female emancipation to the House of Lords

1853 Act for Better Prevention and Punishment of Aggravated Assaults Upon Women and Children: a husband convicted of beating his wife could receive £20 fine or six months 'with or without hard labour'. Following this Act, public debates held on whether a husband should be flogged not jailed/fined. Most convicted men were working class

1853 Charitable Trusts Act: founded the Charity Commission

1854 Scottish Registration Act: births, marriages and deaths recorded. Civil Registration in Ireland fully introduced, 1864

1857   Court of Probate Act, January 1858. Transferred
        responsibility of granting probate to a Principal Probate
        Registry in London and district probate registries.
        National Probate Calendar 1858–1966 is on Ancestry
        and FindMyPast with free service for 1858–1996 at
        https://probatesearch.service.gov.uk/#calendar

1857   Divorce and Matrimonial Causes Act (in force 1 January
        1858) introduced *judicial divorce* when men need only cite
        adultery; wives to prove cruelty or desertion: *judicial
        separation* where a wife can keep her earnings; protection
        for deserted wives; provision for children's custody,
        maintenance and education by the divorce court. Divorce
        possible without an individual Act of Parliament

1857   Industrial Schools Act. Magistrates sent homeless
        children aged 7 to 14 to learn a trade.
        Extended 1861 to include out of control children, beggars,
        those associating with reputed thieves and those without
        visible means of support

1857–64 *English Woman's Journal* launched debating women's
        employment and equality. Edited by Emily Faithfull (1835–
        95) after 1860; she employed women. Original price 1s

1860   Florence Nightingale founds nursing school at St Thomas'
        Hospital, London

1861   Offences Against the Person Act; illegal to marry if
        married to someone else: self-abortion or performing an
        abortion punishable by life imprisonment. See 1967

1864   Contagious Diseases Acts (amended 1866, 1869;
        repealed 1886). Unaccompanied women in port towns
        stopped and forcibly examined for venereal disease

1865   Elizabeth Garrett (1836–1917) first woman to qualify as a
        doctor and included on Medical Register. First practice, 20
        Upper Berkeley Street, London, 1873. First woman to
        achieve membership of British Medical Association

1865   Death of military surgeon Dr James Barry, formerly
        Inspector General HM Military Hospitals – discovered to
        have been a woman (Margaret Ann Bulkely)

1866 Industrial Schools Act set up schools training wayward, homeless or uncontrollable children for a trade

1867 Factory Acts (Extension)/Workshop Regulation Act applied to *all* factories employing more than fifty people: working hours restricted to twelve a day for women and young people; lunchtime break to last one and a half hours; children 8–13 to work half-time; women, children and young people to finish work by 2 p.m. Saturdays; child employees to attend school ten hours a week. Difficult to enforce

1867 Representation of the People Act afforded more men the right to vote (through property)

1867 20 May. First debate on Votes for Women in the House of Commons. Led by John Stuart Mill following a petition by Lady Amberley and Millicent Fawcett. Transcript at *www.historyofwomen.org/1867debate.html*

1869 Emily Davies founds college for female students. Relocates to Girton, Cambridge 1873

1869 Endowed Schools Act; the 1868 Taunton Report enumerated just thirteen girls' secondary schools for the entire country. Following the Act, which set up provision for endowed schools, over ninety girls' grammar schools were established albeit fee paying. A list of endowed schools for England and Wales is found on Wikipedia. The Endowed School Commission merged into Charity Commission, 1974

1869 Municipal Franchise Act gave vote to unmarried or widowed women rate-payers in local elections. Women could serve as Poor Law Guardians and school board members. Local government opportunities for female emancipists

1870 Married Women's Property Act; ensured money earned by married women not appropriated by her husband; see 1882

1870 National Union of Elementary Teachers formed Kings College, London, 25 June 1870, six months before the 1870

Elementary Education Act. Teachers' pay commensurate with pupils' examination results

1870 Elementary Education Act (Forster Act): all children to receive compulsory education from 5 to 13. Charged fees, but school boards to pay for children in poverty: half-time system for children aged 10–14 working in textile industries. Board schools set up in areas without sufficient schools but not in areas deemed to have enough provision
Unmarried women who paid rates could vote for and serve on school boards

1872 Girls Public Day School Company founded. Fees charged c25 guineas a term

1872 Women's Disabilities Removal Bill; Jacob Bright's attempt to give a parliamentary vote to women occupying and owning property failed. Another bid March 1874

1872/3 Bastardy Laws Amendment Acts: attempt to rationalise status of illegitimate children

1872 Infant Life Protection Act: attempt to regulate fostering and 'baby farming' to reduce child mortality

1873 Infant Custody Act promoted custody as needs of child rather than rights of either parent.
Mothers could petition for custody or access to children under 16

1874 Birth and Death Registration Act – compulsory to register a birth. Up to this date, many parents believed a baptised child needn't be formally registered as well. Death supported by medical certificate

1874 Factory Act: minimum age for half-time textile workers is 9; full-time age is 14 with exemption for 13 year olds with minimum education standard; women and children in textile industry restricted to ten hours a day between 6 a.m. and 6 p.m.; working week reduced to fifty-six and a half hours

1874 Manchester Association for Promoting the Education of Women founded

1875   Public Health Act. Public toilet provision for men ('improper' for women to use public facilities). Urban street lighting provided; rubbish removed by councils. New housing to be well-built with internal drainage system and water supply

1876   Medical Act: British medical authorities licensed qualified doctors regardless of gender. Women officially trained and able to practise as doctors. Queen Victoria privately objected to this Act

1878   Factory and Workshops Act. No woman to work more than sixty hours a week. No child under 10 to work. Tighter laws on safety, ventilation and mealtimes. Covered all factories and workshops with inspectors to ensure compliance

1880   Elementary Education Act: school compulsory for children aged 5 to 10; employers of children under 13 must have certificate verifying minimum educational standard

1880   Manx Election Act granted suffrage to women on the Isle of Man to freeholders, later to female householders

1882   Married Women's Property Act enabled women to inherit and own their own property rather than have it appropriated by husband on marriage

1884   Matrimonial Causes Act abolished imprisonment of wives denying her husband conjugal rights. Grounds of petition for divorce see Hansard at *http://hansard.millbanksystems. com/commons/1937/apr/16/clause-2-grounds-of-petition-for-divorce#S5CV0322P0_19370416_HOC_53*

1884   Criminal Law Amendment Bill (Criminal Law Amendment Act, 1885). Following campaign by Josephine Butler and William Thomas Stead (editor of *Pall Mall Gazette*), age of consent for girls raised from 13 to 16. Previously, it was 14 for boys and 12 for girls. Attempt to set up homes for girls under the age of 16/18 begging on streets or working as prostitutes

1888   Bryant & May match-girls' strike

1888   Local Government Act; women can vote for, but not stand as county councillors

1889   Women's Franchise League formed to enfranchise married women. Spinsters and widows already had this right (see 1869)

1890   New Hospital for Women, Euston Road, London, opened. Renamed Elizabeth Garrett Anderson Hospital, 1918

1891   Factory and Workshop Act prohibited factory owners from employing women within four weeks of giving birth

1891   Elementary Education Act raised age of factory half-timers to 11 and provided free compulsory education to all

1893   Elementary Education Act. School leaving age raised to 11. Mothers prohibited from returning to work until eleven weeks after birth

1894   Local Government Act; single and married women with specific property qualification could vote for and stand as parish and district councillors

1897   National Union of Women's Suffrage Societies (NUWSS) founded with seventeen regional societies. Millicent Fawcett, President

1897   Infant Life Prevention Act passed following execution of prolific baby farmer Amelia Dyer. Local authorities to be notified within forty-eight hours of death of any child under 7. Children at risk immediately removed to place of safety

1899   School leaving age, 12

1901   Education (Scotland) Act, Scottish school leaving age, 14

1902   Balfour Education Act abolished board schools; schools under jurisdiction of Local Authorities

1902   Midwives Act. Midwives to be trained, qualified and certified, and enrol with new Central Midwives Board (CMB) by 1910

1903   Emmeline Pankhurst forms Women's Social and Political Union (WSPU) in Manchester

1904   Shops Act limits young people under 18 to seventy-four-hour working week

1904   Ladies' Automobile Club holds first meeting, Duchess of Sutherland, President. Names and addresses of first members listed in Grace's Guide
www.gracesguide.co.uk/1904_Ladies_Automobile_Club

1906   Education (Provision of Meals) Act introduced school dinners

1906   National Federation of Women Workers established

1907   Marriage to Deceased Wife's Sister Act permits a widower to marry his sister-in-law

1907   Qualification of Women Act; women can sit as councillors, aldermen, mayors or chairman on country or borough councils

1907   Education (Administrative Provisions) Act gives free scholarships for promising children at elementary schools to attend secondary school. Grant-aided secondary schools to admit free scholars who have spent two years at public elementary school. Schools received £5 for each child

1907   Formation of Women's Freedom League; breakaway group from WSPU

1908   First UK woman mayor: Dr Elizabeth Garrett Anderson, Aldeburgh, Suffolk

1908   Incest Act defines incest as a crime

1908   Suffragette Edith New chains herself to railings outside 10 Downing Street

1908   Old Age Pensions Act introduced means tested/sliding-scale pensions from 1909 for those aged over 70. Maximum 5s a week for those on an income of less than £21 a year. Nothing for those with an income above £31 10s. Recipients must have been UK resident for twenty years, never imprisoned or holding convictions for insobriety, or purposely impoverished in order to receive the pension. Lives vastly improved

1910   Girl Guide movement founded by Robert Baden Powell (first Boy Scout rally 1909)

1911   Shops Act; shops to close for half a day mid-week i.e. early closing day. Sixty-hour maximum working week. Washing facilities provided for employees

1911 National Health Insurance Act 1911; compulsory insurance for lower paid workers.
Applied to wage earners not their families, e.g. workers received 30s maternity benefit for a child. Women, i.e. domestic servants, generally not covered. Amended 1922 (not for the better). See *www.nationalarchives.gov.uk/ cabinetpapers/themes/health-provision-until-1945.htm* re health provision

1913 Mental Deficiency Act; some women admitted to 'mental institutions' for bearing an illegitimate child

1913 Cat and Mouse Act gave hunger-striking prisoners (suffragettes) temporary discharge for ill health

1918 'Fisher Act:' school leaving age, 14. Abolished half-timers system but this continued into early 1920s

1918 Representation of the People Act. Married women over 30 awarded vote if she or her husband met a property qualification or she had a university degree. 8.5 million women eligible

1918 Qualification of Women Act. Women over 21 allowed to stand as MPs. Seventeen women stood in December general election. Constance Markievicz, Sinn Fein, first woman elected to the Commons but did not take her seat

1919 Nancy Astor, Viscountess Astor, first woman MP elected to the House of Commons (Conservative, Plymouth Sutton)

1919 Sex Disqualification (Removal) Act: unlawful to discriminate against a woman, allowed women into the professions but not to sit in the House of Lords

1921 Deceased Brother's Widow's Marriage Act: widows could marry her brother-in-law

1923 Matrimonial Causes Act: adultery by husband or wife sole ground for divorce

1925 Widows', Orphans and Old Age Contributory Benefits
      Act: 10s a week for life or until remarriage
1926 Legitimacy Act: legitimised children born out of wedlock
      if parents subsequently marry
1926 Births and Deaths Registration Act ensured registration of
      stillborn children
1927 Adoption of Children Act: adoption in England and Wales
      a legal process from 1 January 1927
1928 Equal Franchise Act enables all women over 21 to vote
      in the UK. Fifteen million women eligible
1929 General Election 30 May: women aged between 21 and
      29 vote for the first time
1929 Age of Marriage Act: 16 is minimum age for both sexes
1946 National Health Service introduced: everyone receives
      free medical treatment regardless of ability to pay. In
      force 5 July 1948
1967 Abortion Act
1970 Equal Pay Act

The *www.historyofwomen.org/timeline.html* covers 1520 to 1979.

INDEX